TOO TRUE

Essays on Photography

Also By K. B. Dixon:

Notes
Novel Ideas
The Photo Album
The Ingram Interview
A Painter's Life
Andrew (A to Z)
The Sum of His Syndromes
My Desk and I

TOO TRUE

Essays on Photography

by

K.B. DIXON

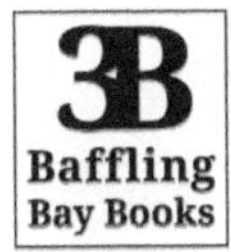

3B

Baffling Bay Books

Cover and interior design by Masha Shubin | www.inkwaterpress.com

The following essays appeared, sometimes in a different form, in the following publications: "Not So Quick in *Wilderness House Literary Review,* "Lucida and Me" in *The Writing Disorder,* "Posing a Question" in *Cobalt Review,* "Hats" in *The Oregonian,* "Captions: A Short Story" in *Maudlin House,* "The Photographic Journal" in *Oregon ArtsWatch,* "The Author Photo" in *The Oregonian,* "A Visible Vivian" in *The Wayne Literary Review.* Photographs Copyright © 2018 by K.B. Dixon kbdixonimages.com

Publisher: Baffling Bay Books

ISBN 978-1-7346759-7-9

1 3 5 7 9 10 8 6 4 2

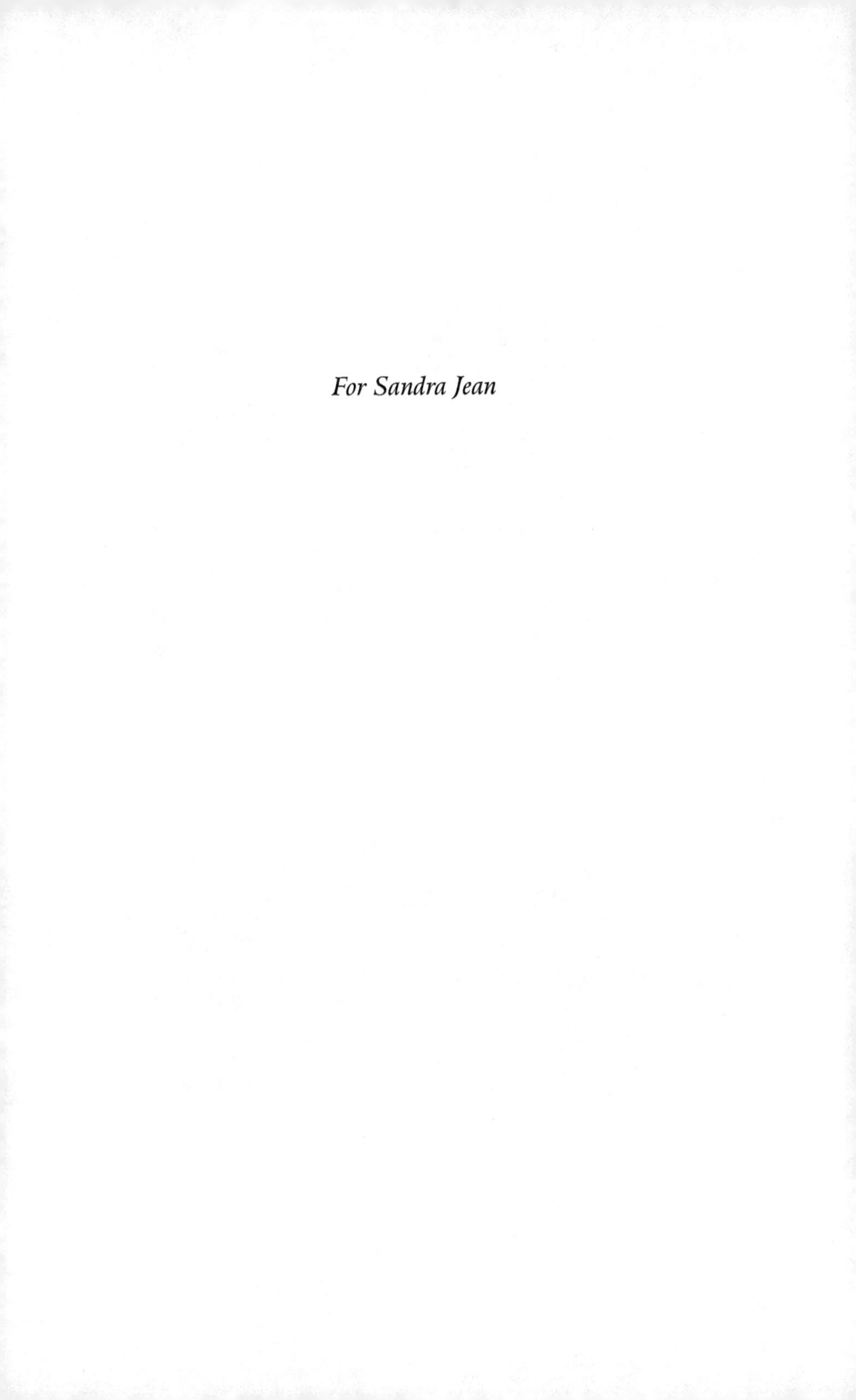

For Sandra Jean

CONTENTS

LIST OF PHOTOGRAPHS

"There is a terrible truthfulness about photography.
The ordinary academician gets hold of a pretty
model, paints her as well as he can, calls her
Juliet, and puts a nice verse from Shakespeare
underneath, and the picture is admired beyond
measure. The photographer finds the same pretty
girl, dresses her up and photographs her, and calls
her Juliet, but somehow it is no good—it is still Miss
Wilkins, the model. It is too true to be Juliet."

George Bernard Shaw, *Wilson's
Photographic Magazine*, LVI, 1909

NOT SO QUICK

Notes on *The Photo Album*

SEVERAL YEARS AGO I WROTE A SHORT, UNCONVENTIONAL novel titled *The Photo Album*. It was a catalogue of imaginary photographs, an idiosyncratic mix of character study and meditation—a glimpse into the life of a peculiar photographer named Michael Quick and a questioning, if somewhat cursory, examination of the medium. It was a work of fiction, and while many of this fictional character's attitudes toward photography were my own, many were not. There has been over time some confusion about this. People familiar with the book have assumed they are familiar with my feelings about the medium, and I have on more than a few occasions been compelled to defend or to disavow Mr. Quick's musings. As time has gone on I have felt more keenly a certain pressure to clarify my position in relation to his, to discuss both our agreements and our disagreements.

The book is divided into 120 short chapters—some

are a sentence or two, others a paragraph, still others a page or two. At the top of each chapter is a graphic— an empty picture frame, a numbered "plate" that holds the imaginary photograph described or alluded to in the text below it. This text carries both the story of the narrator's life as well as his ruminations on the nature of photography.

GUM-CHEWING

In his introduction to *The Photo Album* Mr. Quick informs us that he has been getting serious about photography—or, as he says, getting serious about it again. One of the problems with getting serious about it, he says, "is that at some point in the process ... you will find yourself thinking more than you would like to about the subject of photography in general—about the recalcitrant mystery of it: what it is, what it should be, how it should best be done. It is grueling and ultimately profitless, this noetic gum-chewing."

I understand and sympathize to a degree with my ersatz doppelganger, but I do not feel this way myself. I do not find thinking about the subject of photography to be "noetic gum-chewing." I find it (in measured doses) to be both diverting and exhilarating. I do, however, worry I may be thinking too much about it—that I might be following my inclinations down an analytical rabbit hole.

The poet Phillip Larkin was once asked to write a brief statement of his views on poetry. He did so grudgingly. He did not, he said, find theorizing on the subject any help to him as a poet—and, in fact, he had avoided it as best he could out of concern for his art. It was one thing for a commentator to dissect an impulse, something else entirely for a practitioner. Trying to analyze a photograph is like trying to analyze a joke: the fundamentals may be illuminated, but what is essential will not survive. I am wary of what I recognize in myself as a predisposition—I don't want a set of abstractions, however seductive, mediating my responses to the visual world.

SNAPSHOT

I have never been an advocate of the "snapshot" aesthetic. I have some sympathy for it—especially insofar as it is a reaction to the contrived and airless alternative so popular with a certain downtown crowd—but I find most of these sorts of pictures interesting only as illustrations of a theory, a theory that seems to me conceived in desperation.

I would say the indomitable Mr. Quick and I are in essential agreement here.

I like this aesthetic's commitment to the everyday and to photography's unique relationship to reality, but I do not share its suspicion of thoughtfulness. There is a religious reverence for the spontaneous at the center of this aesthetic, an anti-art bias that conveniently discounts talent and tribulation. While there are things I like about some of these sorts of photographs—their vitality, their immediacy—there are two things in particular about this idealization of the impulse that trouble me. One is its anti-intellectual nature. The other is a certain piety at the heart of this cult—the feeling that the spontaneous, predominantly unmediated response to certain visual sensations captures something primal and authentic and that this primal, authentic thing lends the resulting photograph a certain sort of moral authority. This romantic conception of the impulse is noble-savage nonsense. It fails to take into account or simply ignores the many dubious sources of impulse and the many complex sources of authenticity. It feels false, facile, self-aggrandizing.

SUFFERING

> *Like many, I am attracted to the strange beauty of ruination, to the visceral effects of the peeling-paint picture. My inclination is to prefer those that allude to a metaphysical rather than a sociological subject— pictures about loss, decay, and the passing of time as opposed to those about deprivation and injustice.*

Here Mr. Quick has spoken for me once again. My inclination is to photograph things that interest me psychologically, things that interest me graphically or aesthetically. I do not photograph things that interest me politically or sociologically. I do not, as a rule, go to art to be lectured about poverty, genocide, or environmental depredation. I go other places for that—places where these lectures belong. I go to art for an aesthetic experience, for hope, for pleasure, for insight, for sustenance so that I may find a way to endure the reality of poverty, genocide, and environmental depredation. I leave the photography of suffering to others—to optimists, to sadists, to idealists, to propagandists, to people with a mission, to photojournalists. While there are exceptions (ordinary and extraordinary ones), I see this sort of work more often than not as exploitation—a sort of business decision rather than a testimonial act of empathy.

My own photographs, which are essentially done in the documentary mode, are not done in service to a cause, but as acts of preservation and personal expression. I have tried to capture the outline of what is for me a meaningful moment. I do not have a reformer's bone in my body. My wife, on the other hand, has approximately 206.

STYLE

Style is a perennial problem in photography—that is, individual style. There isn't much room for it. One's choices in style—the varieties and variations—are severely limited by the medium, which is why "subject" almost invariably ends up becoming so important to the intrepid practitioner. It is much easier to make a subject your own than a style—down-and-out farmers, for example, or circus freaks.

Here Mr. Quick is a little too quick for me. I agree in part with what he is saying, but I don't think he has said nearly enough on the subject to serve as a suitable proxy.

Style is indeed, as Mr. Quick observes, a perennial problem in photography. For me there are essentially two types—one that is imposed on a photograph (for a myriad of reasons, usually mercantile) and another that arises organically from a photographer's conscious and unconscious predispositions. The imposed style—a thing formulated to be consistent and easily recognizable—is basically a branding exercise. It's good for business, a way of claiming celebrity status for the photographer. It has nothing to do with modes of expression and everything to do with getting noticed, with catching the "right someone's eye," with turning a gimmick into money—into a house in the Hamptons, into a mention in *The New York Times*.

The organic style is subtler in most cases, a thing that emerges naturally over time. If there is calculation, it is about basic composition. Each photograph is a report on the photographer. It contains trace amounts of a unique temperament. It is like an answer on the MMPI (Minnesota Multiphasic Personality Inventory)—a singular clue that when put together with other singular clues provides a sense of the complex consciousnesses behind them. It is a style that is naturally reductive rather than artificially so—constrained by the limitations of the photographer as opposed to constrained by the demands of the art market.

The style Mr. Quick is talking about as being "limited by the medium" is the imposed style. This has led him, I think, to overestimate the importance of the subject and to underestimate the importance of the photographer. The subject of a photograph plays one role in the imposed style, another in the organic. In the imposed style it is evidence of what a photographer thinks someone else might be interested in whereas in the organic style it offers evidence of what the photographer himself is interested in. Both, of course, offer coded commentaries. The emphasis placed on these two things—subject and manner—is divided more evenly in photography than in painting. I do not share Mr. Quick's feelings of an inherent bias.

MANIPULATION

As a rule I try to keep my postproduction manipulations of the image to a minimum. I will crop, I will adjust both white balance and color, I will sharpen, I will occasionally do a little dodging and burning— that is about it. I have never been able to fully equate technical manipulations with imaginative ones.

Mr. Quick and I are very much on the same page here.

I have little interest in digitally manipulated images— photographs that are not photographs. I am not talking about basic digital darkroom manipulations—the adjustments Mr. Quick refers to (exposure, white balance, the excision of dust spots, etc.), but the wholesale transformation of images. I'm talking about composites, collages, constructions—about additions and subtractions, imported backgrounds, fakery, anything that degrades a photograph's "adherence" to its referent (if you'll excuse the stupefying art-speak). In short, I'm talking about photographs that are fictions. Both those that are obviously so, and most particularly those that are surreptitiously so— those that are conscious deceits. My interest is in capture, not confabulation; in the real world, not in still photography's "special effects." The further a photograph moves away from its realist roots—the source of its greatest strength, its magic—the less my interest. Crossing over from the actual to the conceptual is not for me a way of legitimizing the medium, but a way of addressing status anxiety. It is a way of claiming for oneself the prestigious title of "artist" as opposed to the considerably less glamorous one of "photographer." A photograph is a miracle. There is no need to apologize for it not being a painting.

STATEMENTS

This picture is included not so much for its subject or its formal qualities as for its relationship to a fleeting sense I had of myself as a photographer. If you are going to get all serious about it—and I'm not sure that I think you should—a photograph is an admission by the photographer that however much he might prefer to equivocate, this is something he has found engaging.

Mr. Quick's parenthesis here bothers me. People mistake his tentativeness for mine. I have no doubt that photography is something to be serious about. I understand, however, Mr. Quick's wariness of the crowing photographer—the photographer who wears his seriousness like a sandwich board. Mr. Quick has, I believe, read a few too many "artist's statements." I try to stay away from them. I have never read one that made me like the artist or the artist's work more, but many that made me like him, her, or it less. I believe naively that an image should speak for itself. If it requires a caption or a statement it is not a photograph—it is an illustration. In most cases these statements are nothing more than polysyllabic sales pitches—efforts not so much to explicate or to inform as to present the artist as someone substantive and profound—in other words, a good investment.

THE ORDINARY

What sort of pictures do I take? I would say in general that I stay away from both the sublime and the ridiculously ordinary—in part because they have both been so hopelessly overdone, but also because I have an obdurate predisposition to be suspicious of extremes. In the beginning when I did list in one direction or the other, it was, of course, more likely to be toward the sublime than toward the subtexturally encrusted antithesis, but lately this has changed. Exploring the quintessentially common is a tricky thing to do right—it requires greater foresight and additional technical expertise—but I have found myself getting more and more interested in trying it.

I would say that here Mr. Quick and I are in agreement yet again. I have, as of late, sensed a growing interest in the "portentous significance" of the ordinary. I have a feeling, however, that Mr. Quick may be—at the moment anyway—a little farther down this road than me.

REPRESENTATION

This shot of an unassuming brass table lamp is as emotionally neutral as I could make it. A simple statement of fact, I think of it as a sort of ode to representation—a comment on the banality of the phantasmagoric, on the changing image-landscape super-saturated as it is with computer-generated inventions where the fantastic has become a stale bore and the quotidian an endangered exotic.

I share completely Mr. Quick's terse assessment of the contemporary image landscape. (See "Manipulation.")

STREET PEOPLE

This is another photo taken for my Portland, Inside and Out project. The subject is one of our colorfully disturbed street people. I have not taken many of these sorts of pictures because I cannot shake the feeling that they are exploitive. It would be silly to pretend that I do not find these marginalized people fascinating, but I am just not prepared very often to try this sort of thing. I have never been able to convince myself that I am doing it for the right reasons—that I am in some way providing an introductory service, embracing a difficult diversity, celebrating a broader view of humanity rather than simply trading on a prurient and callous curiosity. These people are easy subjects—they provide even the most mediocre photographer with credentials as a sophisticate, but these sorts of shots are not what they used to be. The elevating audacity was drained out of them decades ago. While I do think these sorts of pictures can make a valuable point about alienation, about isolation, about suffering, about the nature of the human condition, most of them don't. The respect repeatedly declared for the subject invariably seems more perfunctorily prescribed than sincere.

Yes, Mr. Quick is speaking for me here. (See "Suffering.")

INDELIBLE

One of the peculiar things about a photo is its afterlife. Photos are, as a rule, relatively quick and easy—quick and easy to take, quick and easy to take in. However good, one spends only a fraction of the time with a photograph that one spends with a painting. The irony, of course, is that the image (if not the feeling) may be more indelibly imprinted, may last longer.

Like Mr. Quick, I am fascinated by the way we remember a photograph. I agree with maybe 50% of what he is saying here. When he is talking about taking a photograph, he is talking about taking a photograph in general, I believe—not about taking a "good" photograph. That is something else entirely. Quick and easy it is not.

BEAUTY

I experienced this as an exquisitely beautiful scene— that is to say, the sort of thing one usually sees only in photographs—so I took the picture. We were in San Diego. We went to Balboa Park. I turned around and there was this mission steeple framed perfectly by palm trees and blooming hedges. If you were to say this picture was merely beautiful, I would agree with you. Like most people, I have seen too many beautiful photographs—I have become desensitized. This does not mean I do not want to see more or occasionally try to make one myself—I do.

Here Mr. Quick and I part ways a bit. I think I am less interested than him in looking at or making conventionally beautiful photographs. Sunsets and seascapes are for me the visual equivalent of elevator music. They are placemats and postcards.

TIME

> *There is something uniquely attractive about the geometric form. There is a rightness and wrongness to it—a rectilinear precision—that is not present in the biomorphic form. As I have said, I indulge myself periodically. I enjoy taking these sort of pictures more than I enjoy looking at them. They are usually of interest to me only briefly. I do not see them as intellectual or emotional communications—I see them simply as optical exercises and/or symbols of a cold and sanitary style.*

Mr. Quick and I are in complete agreement here except I think I like the occasional abstract image just the slightest bit more than him. This does not mean, however, that I am regularly engaged by abstraction. I am not. These sorts of images can be graphically interesting, but they are not photographically interesting. They are missing what is for me one of the central elements of the medium—time.

Whatever else a photograph may do, it invariably preserves for us the slightest snip of time—the ghost of that millisecond just past, the radial reflection of an actual existence. This temporality is at the heart of photography. A photograph that ignores this ignores the essence of the medium. There is a quality I have heard described as well as it can be of "thereness" to a good photograph. It puts you in direct visual and visceral contact with a person, place, or thing that is physically and temporally distant from you. These photographs ripen with age—the temporal distance becomes more dramatic with each passing year. It adds to a photograph's value as a document and as an aesthetic object.

My problem with abstract images is the same as my problem with most landscape images. They are timeless—or are supposed to be. They do not ripen. I am not particularly interested in a photograph of a mountain range taken in 1865, but a storefront, a shopkeeper, or a soldier—that is different. For me photography can be about a lot of things, but it is always to some degree about time. Time and light.

TRIVIALITIES

I like this simple little shot—this isolated sliver of reality that is normally overlooked. Teasing the meaning from apparent trivialities—it is one of the things that photography does so well.

We agree again, Mr. Quick and I. As he said elsewhere in his introduction, "there doesn't seem to be anything [the camera] cannot make interesting." This is both a blessing and a curse. It is one thing to tease the meaning from apparent trivialities and another thing to make apparent trivialities appear meaningful. Not every mundanity contains a marvel. Some trivialities are, in fact, just trivialities. When the camera suggests otherwise, it misleads.

DESCRIPTION

If I were interested in this photograph being considered a work of art, I would have had to deny the debt it owes to its subject. I would have had to insist on the primacy of a personal vision, claim that what has been presented is an esoteric interpretation of light and space or an expressive evocation of some sort of metaphysical mood. There is no idea more insidious, more responsible for crap pictures than the idea that mood or individual interpretation supersedes description. Description—which is at the heart of documentation—is at the heart of photography, and to cavalierly derogate it in favor of a self-aggrandizing aesthetic of visionary license seems to me simply wrong-headed and craven. The fear, of course, is that emphatic description will remind the viewer that the image is the product of a camera when the glory-hunting narcissist would prefer he think it wholly that of a rich imagination.

This passage surprises me. I am very much in agreement with it—I just did not know Mr. Quick had been thinking along these lines. I am wary, of course, of endorsing this paragraph as it is heavily nuanced and requires a careful unpacking. I can see it easily being misunderstood. It is essentially a plea for equal treatment. It does not disparage individual expression, it emphasizes the importance of documentation—the source of photography's power. Mr. Quick is a little strident perhaps in his defense of documentation, but I understand fully his frustration with the coddling conventions of toothless commentary.

PATTERNS

> *I like taking pictures of patterns and do it fairly often, but, as with abstracts, I don't much like looking at them—not for any length of time anyway. I find the remorseless homogeneity of these images initially comforting but ultimately oppressive—more a denigration of the individual and the authentic than a celebration of the many and the fecund.*

Like Mr. Quick, I enjoy photographing patterns, but I would have to say that on this subject his thinking is a little more advanced than mine. My interests tend to be more in the graphic issues than in the philosophical.

ART

> *Is photography art? This was apparently a question for debate until just recently. According to the professoriate the question has been answered in the affirmative by institutional consensus. Personally I am not so sure. (I am also not so sure it actually matters.) That photography has had the title conferred on it is obviously true, but with contemporary curatorial silliness running the polished hallways of power unchecked, the authority of these institutions to make this conferment has been rightly called into question. I know photographers would like it to be considered "art," would like to have their names decorated with the designation, but it seems to me an overly broad use of the word. Referring to a photographer as an "artist" is like referring to a musician as one; it may be loosely accurate, but it doesn't really seem to be*

strictly the case. The appellation seems more a complex species of honorifica than a statement of fact.

This section of this peculiar little book (and one in which Mr. Quick refers to photography as a "peripheral art form" that was "maybe on a par with dance") has caused me considerable trouble. We agree about the manipulated image for the most part, but his opinions on photography as "art" are entirely his own. The stance he has taken is, I believe, purposefully provocative. It is one he was obliged to take for "dramatic reasons" by a manipulative author, so I am not going to hold it against him—not entirely. Photography for me is quite obviously an art. It is a new art, not a peripheral one. Where it ranks in the hierarchy of arts has yet to be determined. The struggle for status (and its accompanying financial rewards) has just begun. The most impassioned advocates seem to be those who are trying to monetize the medium. I have none of Mr. Quick's trepidations.

STREET PHOTOGRAPHY

For all of its attraction, there is a quality to some street photography that I have a little trouble with: its unrelieved earnestness. I can take this occasionally like cough syrup and benefit, but too much of it upsets my stomach. I prefer my pictures a little less sanctimonious, my photographers a little less certain of their own good intentions and privileged access to the truth.

I have to agree with my struggling double that this is a frequent problem.

THUMBPRINT

Larkin wrote poems, he said, to preserve things he had seen, thought, and felt both for himself and for others, but that his first responsibility was to the experience itself, which he sought to keep from oblivion for its own sake. I must admit a cynic's inclination to distrust all proclamations of altruistic motivation. I think this "art for art's sake" trope is and always was something of an esoteric dodge. The experience may have intrinsic value and deserve saving "for itself," but it has always had an attractive ancillary value as well. What Larkin sought to save from oblivion was not only the experience, but evidence of the experience's experiencer—the perceiving consciousness. I think this is very much the case for Mr. Quick and me. In addition to documenting a very small part of the world around us, we are hoping to preserve for ourselves and others forever a transient moment of aesthetic pleasure, a moment that will by necessity bear however faintly the thumbprint of the experiencing consciousness that just so happens to be him—and me.

I hope this has cleared up at least some of the confusion about Mr. Quick's general attitudes and mine—that it has defined some of our agreements and disagreements. It will not, I am sure, be the last word.

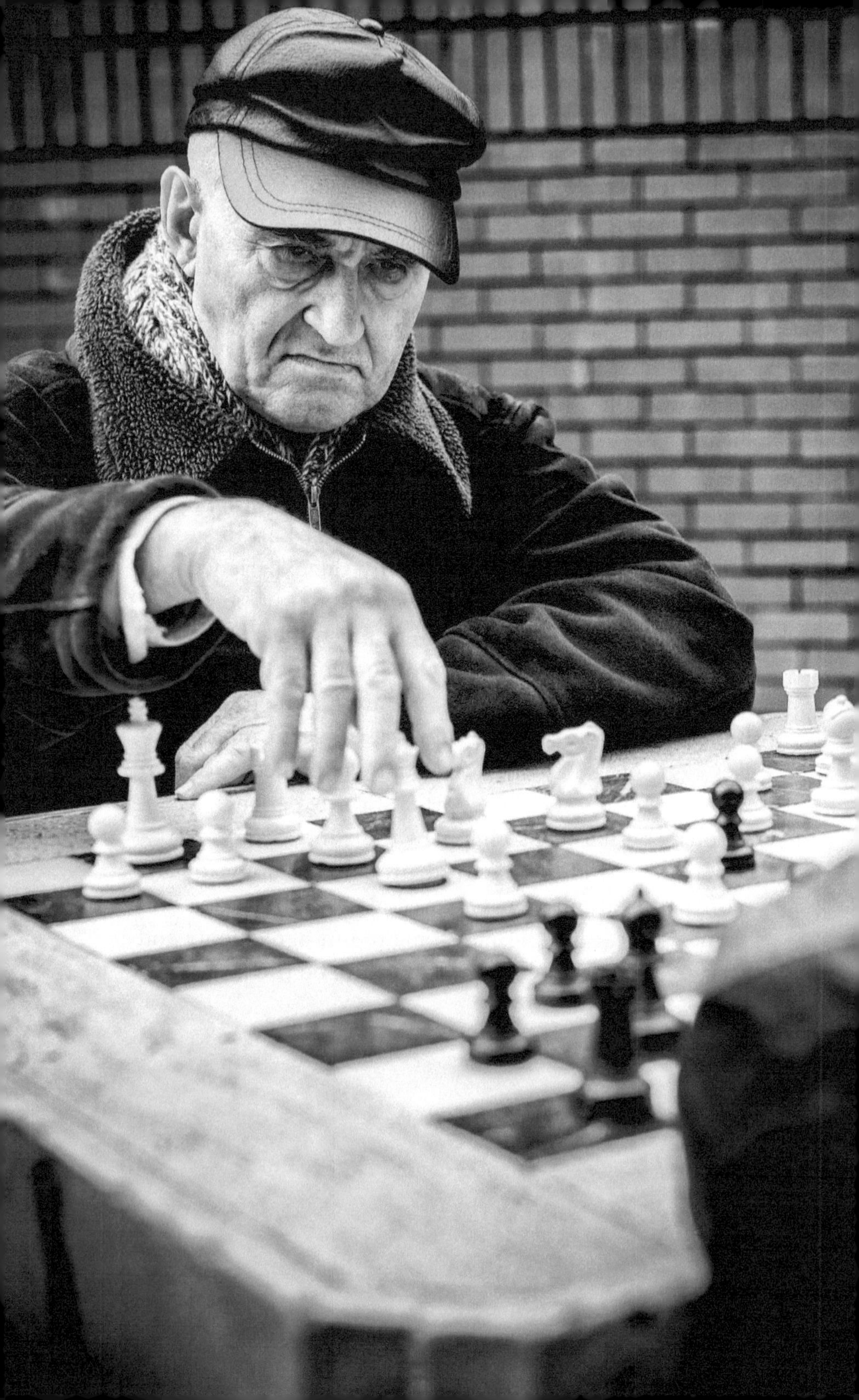

LUCIDA AND ME

ANY PHOTOGRAPHER WHOSE INTEREST IN THE SUBJECT extends to reading more than just his camera manuals will eventually come upon the names Susan Sontag and Roland Barthes. Their books—*On Photography* and *Camera Lucida*—are canonical texts. It is difficult to read anything thoughtful on the subject that does not mention one or the other.

I read the Sontag book many years ago with pleasure, but came reluctantly and late to *Camera Lucida*—reluctantly because it was a translation, late because it was Roland Barthes. As a writer I was—and still am—wary of translation (a subject for another time). As a reader I was wary of Barthes. I had a residual bias against him, a keepsake from college where I and a thousand hapless others were compelled by sadistic professors to read

Photo: Chess Match, 2013

such things as *Writing Degree Zero* and *Elements of Semiology*—a bias against him for the role he played (with Lacan, Foucault, Derrida, *et al.*) as a founding father of "Theory," the torturous gobbledygooking of literary study that did for literary criticism what smallpox did for the Plains Indians.

But in the end I was lured to the book by quotations that I found everywhere and by a promise—a promise that the Barthes of *Lucida* was different from the Barthes of *Image-Music-Text*, *Mythologies*, and *S/Z*; different from the Barthes that Barthes-likers liked, the one euphemistically referred to as "rigorous" (read gratuitously obscure). *Lucida* was shorter, more intimate, more personal than the impenetrable tomes on which his statue stood.

What I found was a book that was technically "as-advertised"—that is, a book that was un-Barthes-like to some degree (but, alas, not to degree zero). It was by most objective standards quite likely the least Barthes-like of Barthes books, but it was not by my troglodytic standards quite un-Barthes-like enough. I found plenty of the old writer here—lapses into the calorieless paragraphs of semiological word-salad that reminded me of why I had avoided him. He talks about being torn between two languages—expressive and critical—about abandoning the latter as "reductive," but he cannot resist the Siren call of an influential constituency clamoring for a bowlful of scholarly jargon. Clarity, it seems, is to be treated as a form of groveling.

Camera Lucida is divided into two parts. Each is itself subdivided into a plethora of short, related sections. Part One examines the subject of photography in general. Part Two circles around a single image. Although Part One was for me the most problematic—the most inclined to empty amplitude—it was not without its points of interest; for instance, Barthes's thoughts about being photographed himself and the famous coinage of "punctum."

Like most people Barthes had a troubled relationship with his photographic image. "Once I feel myself observed by the lens," he wrote, "everything changes...I transform myself in advance into an image." The image he transformed himself into was never satisfactory. "If only I could 'come out' on paper," he writes, "as on a classical canvas, endowed with a noble expression—thoughtful, intelligent, etc! In short...be painted (by Titian) or drawn (by Clouet)!" Barthes being Barthes, he could not admit to the pedestrian vanities that plague we mere mortals. The problem was not that he looked sallow or overweight—it was that his portraitist had not captured "a delicate moral texture." One would have to love him, he quite rightly observed, to see what he would like them to see in a photograph—the "precious essence of [his] individuality." The fault, dear viewer, was not in ourselves that we were underlings, but in the medium that it was not sympathetic. He returns to this subject again and again. That he should address it so early in the book and at such relative length and with such obvious passion says something about its importance to him, and its importance to him is something that should be taken into account when trying to assess the various ambiguities of his wandering analysis.

If Helen's face launched a thousand ships, Barthes's coinage "punctum" launched a thousand tortured essays. It was catnip to the explicating classes, a favorite of fledgling poseurs everywhere. I have always had a problem with it—first as a word, but more importantly as a concept. As a word it has always struck me as unnecessarily ugly. (But then, of course, it may sound sweeter to the classically-educated Francophone's ear than to the State University-educated Anglophone's.) As a concept it has always seemed trite. Early in Part One Barthes takes an analytical axe to his subject (the essence of Photography) and divides it into competing parts: *Studium*, the ostensible subject of the photograph, the source of the viewers "polite" interest, and *Punctum*, a tangential detail that provokes a personal reaction, that breaks through the complacent response, "an accident which pricks." To me this seems an almost meaningless tautology—a needlessly obscure way of saying that certain photographs have a certain something about them that makes them special to certain someones—a commonplace that when draped in Latin becomes a shiny original thing, a breathtakingly sophisticated utterance.

Find the Punctum became a popular game for a while—a *Where's Waldo* for academics. A futile game, I'm afraid. What is punctum? A special something that may not be found in every photograph. What is this special something? It differs from one person to the next. It is a detail that attracts, that moves, that holds. One cannot say why. It is not a general special-somethingness, but a special somethingness that is specifically "special to me." It is, Barthes says, "What I add to a photograph." It is wholly subjective. A punctum is a punctum only to the punctee. Your punctum is not my punctum or X's punctum or Y's or Z's—but hasn't it been a lot of fun going on interminably about it.

The introduction to my copy of *Lucida* was written by the current go-to guy on the subject of photography: the inventive and agile Geoff Dyer. "To formalize…Barthes' argument," he writes at one point, "is not simply to diminish it, but to rob it of so many subtleties as to misrepresent it entirely." This is an artful dodge, a gracious effort by Dyer (a man hired to do a gracious job) to cover for Barthes, to warn us off our bourgeois ways. Barthes is uncomfortable with the exposure lucidity allows. The clearer one's expression, the fewer places there are to hide. One of the important things about this sort of writing—the reason it is obscure—is that it offers a way out. One can always claim to have been misunderstood.

For all the notoriety and thesis-fodder of Part One, it is Part Two of *Lucida* that interests me, that means something to me, that engages me. It is here that Barthes changes rhetorical gears, becomes more personal. Having failed to discover the essential nature of Photography in the previous sixty pages, he proposes to dig deeper into himself to find what he is looking for. It is here that my internal conversation with him changes a little, becomes a little less antagonistic. Here, mixed in with the brilliant claptrap and convolution, is poetry and pathos.

A month after his mother's death Barthes was sitting alone in his apartment (the apartment where she died) sorting through photographs of her. He was struck by the fact that they gave him so little. None of them seemed "right"—that is, none of them seemed to have captured what was essential about her. He continued looking through these photographs one by one "looking for the truth of the face [he] had loved." Finally he found it. He was staggered. It was an old photograph—dog-eared, faded. It showed two children—his mother (age 5) and her brother (age 7) standing at the end of a wooden bridge in a glassed-in conservatory—a "winter garden." The sensation was for him overwhelming. "I studied the little girl and at last rediscovered my mother." In this image he found "the kindness which had formed her being immediately and forever." It is here in this moment when he makes this discovery that I made a discovery of my own, that I suddenly and quite unexpectedly felt a connection to the man—and not just any sort of connection, but a close one. I recognized the sensation he was describing. I had experienced an almost supernaturally similar shock coming across a photograph of my very-much-living wife. That photograph was, likewise, an old one. It sits at this moment about three feet from me in a small, egg-shaped pewter frame. My wife (also age 5) is not standing in a winter garden, but sitting in a winter coat on the knee of a department-store Santa, and I can see in her face the excitement and innocent joy that formed her being immediately and forever. I found in Barthes's lushly described response to this treasured photograph of his an eerie, almost perfect, articulation of my own unarticulated feelings about this treasured photograph of mine—a photograph that has remained for me an emblem of the medium's mystery.

The Winter Garden photograph became a guide for Barthes, the foundation of his thinking on the subject of Photography. "Something like an essence of the Photograph floated in this particular picture," he says of the image. This particular "something-like-an-essence" was the sort of thing one could build a metaphysics of Photography around if they were so inclined. Barthes, of course, was so inclined.

A photograph, Barthes says, is "a mutant…neither image nor reality, a new being, really: a reality one can no longer touch." The photograph "ratifies what it represents." It "can lie as to the meaning of a thing… never as to its existence." In photography one "can never deny that *the thing has been there.*" The essence of Photography is, he says, "that-has-been." As a realist this is a view I endorse—digital-age quibbles aside. Of course, this "that-has-been" idea leads Barthes quickly to a darker place, to the logical and familiar conclusion: "but-is-no-more." In every photograph, he writes, is the "imperious sign" of death—not just any death, but his own. (If Barthes cannot link a thing to "death" or "madness," he does not think he is doing his job.) The theory that evolves circles around the photograph as *memento mori.* "In front of the photograph of my mother as a child, I tell myself: she is going to die: I shudder…*over a catastrophe which has already occurred.*"

In photographs "there is always a defeat of Time... *that* is dead and *that* is going to die." He observes with "horror" this "anterior future." The experience of time defeated is dizzying. He is mesmerized (as I am) by the medium's unique ability to mix the past, the present, and the future—what has been, what is now, what will be. I share his fascination with time in a photograph (if not his inclination to morbidity). For me a good photograph is made of time, light, and feeling. There is no question that it is a melancholic medium—to experience it as a tragic one requires a certain exertion and a certain predisposition.

Barthes returns in his exposition to the Winter Garden image. It fascinates him. He lingers over it just as I linger over my Santa picture. "The photograph," he writes, "is literally an emanation of the referent." These emanations are "a sort of umbilical cord," he says, that "links the body of the photographed thing to [his] gaze." "Hence the Winter Garden Photograph, however pale, is for me the treasury of rays which emanated from my mother as a child, from her hair, her skin, her dress, her *gaze, on that day*." A photograph is not just the preservation of a split-second, but of a life, of a "unique being." I have a strong sympathy for this view. But in lingering with it, he is frustrated—he cannot enter the photograph as he would like. "I can only sweep it with my glance," he says. It "arrests" further interpretation—he has exhausted himself with his "*this-has-been*" realization.

Barthes confronts the question again: what is it that makes this special photograph a special photograph? It is something beyond resemblance, something more than physical reality. This mysterious essence-like something is what Barthes calls (with shocking simplicity) the "air" of the photograph. It is another undefinable essential—an unanalyzable thing that is evident but cannot be proven, a secret door through which he can escape troublesome parts of any previous analysis. The "air," he says, "is the luminous shadow which accompanies the body." He returns yet again to photographs of himself. Without this shadow, the subject does not come to life. This is what is wrong with the photographs he has seen of himself: "if these thousand photographs have each 'missed' my air, my effigy will perpetuate my identity, not my value." In other words, we do not have his true image.

The photograph, Barthes says, is "a bizarre medium; a new form of hallucination." This is a nice way to think of it. Likewise, *Lucida* is a bizarre book, a new form of critique. There is a great deal to admire about it—the only problem it seems to me is that most of the admiring being done is being done without reservation. There is a part of me that wishes there was a part of me that cared more about being charitable on the subject of theory-speak. (Who does not want to seem fair-minded?) For me it was (and still is) a lot of sound and fury signifying nothing. It is not about the pursuit of truth or knowledge, but reputation—a status game, its defining high-syllable-count gibberish a sort of tribal patois. Its famous obscurity has nothing to do with subtleties or with the difficulty of the subject and everything to do with ego, fashion, and professional advancement. There is less of this sort of thing in *Lucida* than elsewhere—passages that have been "freed from the tyranny of meaning"—but for me, not less enough. One cannot ignore the grief that is everywhere in this book, and a more conventionally empathetic person than me would, I suspect, be inclined to make greater allowances. I might have made greater allowances myself if I had not been misled into thinking the subject here was to be Photography. *Lucida* is, in fact, only partly about photography—it is in equal parts about how smart Mr. Barthes is and how deeply injured.

From its beginning *Lucida* has provided inspiration and annoyance. A pedigreed consideration of photography's endlessly replicating complexity, it took its subject seriously at a time when it needed to be taken seriously, and in so doing it offered aid and comfort to those championing the medium.

The photograph is not "a 'copy' of reality," Barthes wrote, "but an emanation of *past reality*: a *magic*, not an art." This is one of the quotes that brought me to *Lucida*, that indicated to me a shared sense of the subject. This ends up so many times being, for me, the last word on photography. It is, I think, the best analysis yet of the essence of Photography, a response to the wonder of what may be found in a single image—its ability to transcend time and space, to put one in direct contact with more than just near and distant pasts.

Photo: Woman on Motorcycle, 2013

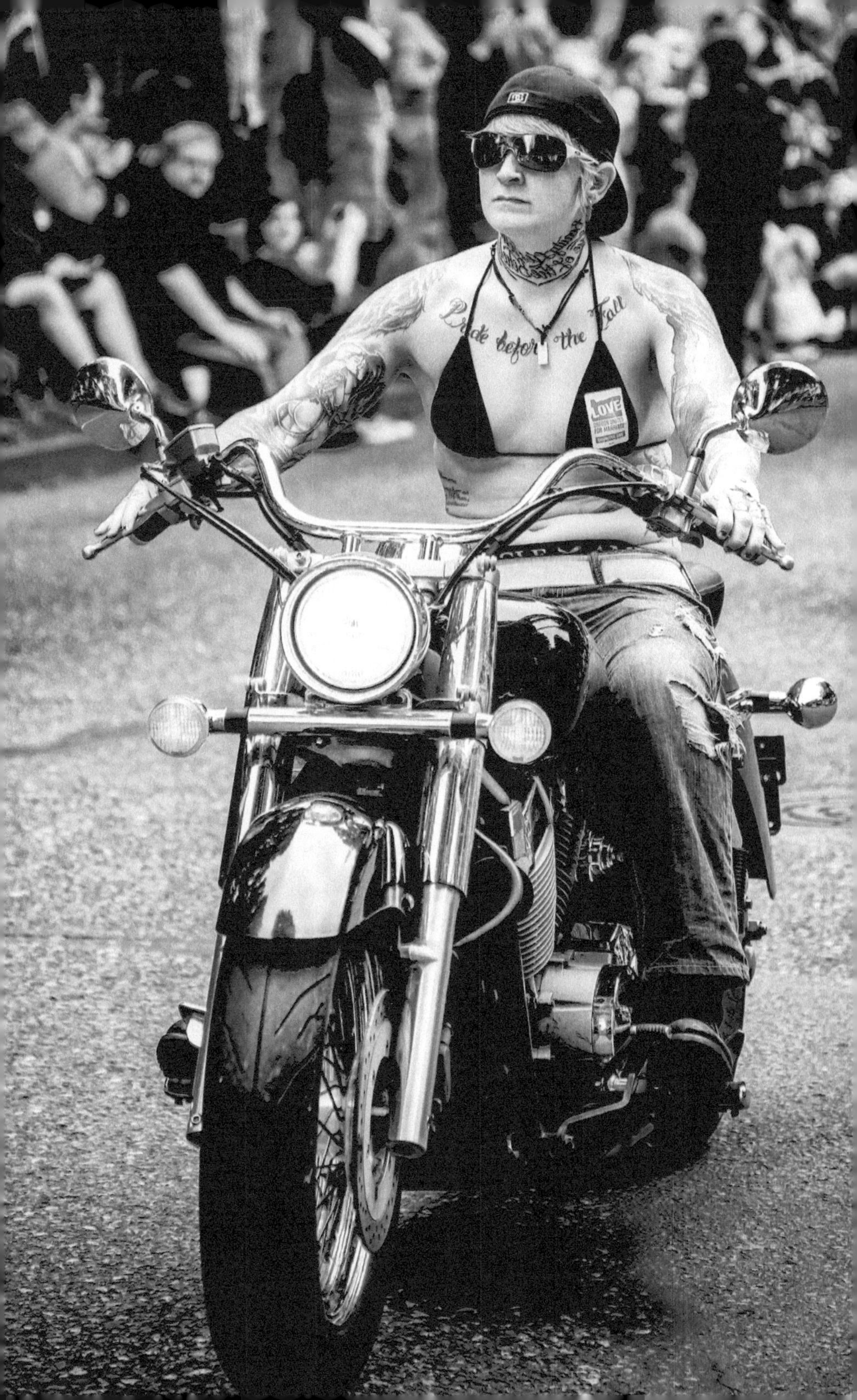

LOVE
FOR MARRIAGE

POSING A QUESTION

PHOTOGRAPHY ESSENTIALLY BEGAN AS THE ART OF PORTRAIture. With the daguerreotype the portrait—previously painted and available only to an aristocratic few— became relatively inexpensive and available to everyone. John Szarkowski, the legendary director, curator, and poohbah-emeritus at New York's Museum of Modern Art, noted in *Looking at Photographs* (his survey of the museum's extensive collection) that "of the countless thousands of daguerreotypes that survive, not one in a hundred shows a building or a waterfall or a street scene." What they show is "an endless parade of ancestors." With the daguerreotype, Szarkowski wrote, "every man's family acquired a visual past...." Not only that, every man acquired for himself a visual present and a knowledge of that present. It is no surprise given the unique fidelity of this new medium that this knowledge produced its own special set of problems with regard to the portrait. In the 1850s Nadar, one of the most famous of the early French photographers, stopped taking photographs of women because the results were, he said, "too true to nature to please the sitters, even the most beautiful." The lines were drawn early on between what the subject wanted in a photograph and what the ambitious photographer wanted. What the subject wanted was, of course, to look good—and not just garden-variety good, but, if possible, better than they had ever looked before. What the ambitious photographer wanted was something else, something important, something vital—they wanted a photograph infused with those qualities that animate a work of art.

The candid portrait—a photograph taken without the subject being aware of it— was pioneered in the early 1900s by Paul Strand, Walker Evans, and others. It was the serious photographer's answer to the sterile studio portrait of the day—the homogenized work aimed primarily at flattering the sitter. Evans's "Subway Portraits" in the 1930s were done with a hidden camera, the lens poking out between the buttons of his overcoat. He described the series as an aesthetic protest against posed portraiture. The idea was that a person captured unaware would reveal something substantive about him or herself, something truthful, something he or she would not reveal if they were conscious of the camera. It is true, of course, that a person will make this sort of revelation; but the obverse is also true—a fact that is generally underappreciated. A person aware of being photographed reveals something substantive about him or herself that he or she would not be revealing if they were unaware and in repose. Unaware, the face reflects the conversation a subject is having with him or herself. Aware, the face reflects a conversation the subject is having with someone else. It gives us different information—information that is frequently more difficult to decode, but no less trustworthy, no less significant.

One of the most famous examples of the candid portrait is Strand's *Blind Woman, New York 1916*—a poignant and desolating image of an aging beggar with a sign hung around her neck identifying her as blind. It is an iconic photograph—one that the critic Geoff Dyer described forensically as the "graphic illustration of the photographer's ideal relationship to his subject." It is obviously an illustration of one relationship, but it is not for me the "ideal" one—it is just one of many. Compare this photograph to another of Strand's famous portraits, *Mr. Bennett, Vermont 1944*. Mr. Bennett is very much aware of the fact that he is being photographed. Does this diminish the photograph's power? No. Does one of these portraits feel more truthful than the other? Not to me. There is an assumption that the candid portrait tells you more than it often does and that the posed photograph tells you less. This assumption rests in large part on a pair of iffy suppositions: one about the nature of solitude (that it is invariably primal and profound), the other about the nature of presentation (the idea that the way one tries to present one's self or succeeds in presenting one's self has nothing to do with who they really are when in fact there can be, in some cases, no better indicator of who a person is than a view of who they think they are or who they want you to think they are).

Over time the logistical and expressive limitations of the candid portrait became obvious. Photographers returned to the posed photograph seeking new ways of getting what they wanted—which was something informative, something meaningful. One strategy (which acknowledged a residual bias in favor of the candid portrait) was to play with the idea of candor by simulating unawareness, by having the sitter pose as if not posing—to appear oblivious, to gaze off somewhere lost in thought, to do something, to be "absorbed" in some action that precluded the subject putting on a face to meet the camera. It is a stratagem on which the garrulous and habitually recursive Michael Fried has opined at length (see, for example, *Absorption and Theatricality*).

Some subjects, of course, are better at this fake unawareness than others, but we as viewers are surprisingly good at detecting this just as we are surprisingly good at making visual assessments of character. It's hardwired. As the photographer Diane Arbus famously noted, there is in the posed photograph "a gap between intention and effect." There is what the sitter wants to tell you and what they may inadvertently reveal. Actors (and sociopaths) can and do exploit this common dissonance.

They study to control this gap—to keep these inadvertent revelations to a minimum. But it's not just actors and sociopaths. More and more everyday people are becoming practiced at this. Photographer Garry Winogrand took photographs, he said, "to find out what something looked like photographed." Today with the proliferation of cameras and the obsessive interest in one's self, everyone knows what they look like photographed. They have been photographed by themselves and others almost since birth. They have developed a posing strategy to make sure they look (as much as possible) the way they want to. It has made it much harder for the ambitious photographer to get a "real" photograph, to mine that discrepancy between intention and effect for the elemental substances they are seeking.

—

As a photographer I have taken portraits and as a writer I have had portraits taken, so I have at least a passing familiarity with both sides of the ongoing struggle for control of the image. There is a quality I have heard described as well as it can be, I think, of "thereness" to a good portrait. It puts the viewer in direct visual contact with a person who is physically and temporally distant from them. It is the type of photograph that ripens—the temporal distance becomes more dramatic with each passing year and adds to the photograph's value as a document and as an aesthetic object. A good portrait is not about faithful transcription, but about faithful representation. It preserves and presents a feeling as well as a form. "In front of the lens, I am at the same time: the one I think I am, the one I want others to think I am, the one the photographer thinks I am, and the one he makes use of to exhibit his art. In other words, a strange action," wrote Roland Barthes. I couldn't agree more with his description of this photographic encounter—"a strange action" to be sure.

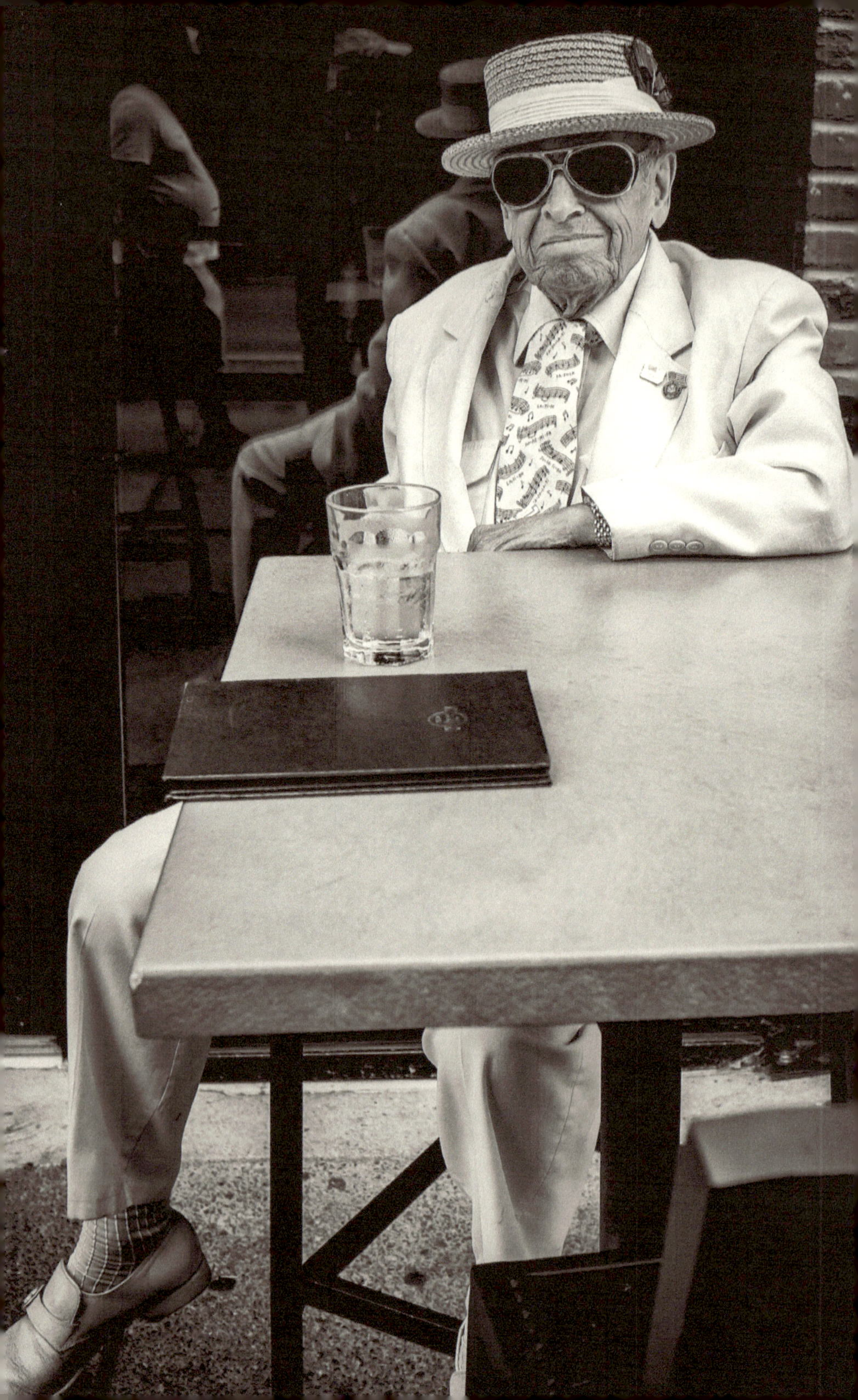

HATS

I DON'T KNOW ABOUT YOUR LIST OF MAGAZINE SUBSCRIP-tions, but mine is long and alive. It expands and contracts spasmodically. Things come and go. Editors change, my tastes change, the times change—there will be something new I want to try and something old I have gotten bored with or tired of. Whatever the vagaries—the additions and subtractions—there are two names that have stayed on this list pretty consistently over the years: *The New Yorker* and *Harper's*. They have their problems from time to time, of course, but they remain on the whole exceptional publications, cultural treasures. There are all sorts of nice things that can and should be said about them, about their contributions to the community, to the contemporary debate, to the life of the mind, but what I want to talk

Photo: Man in White Suit, 2013

about here, in part, are the advertisements—not the big flashy ones that bring in the serious money (the jeweled watches, the investment services, the luxury automobiles, the blood-pressure medications), but the little guys squeezed in at the back of the bus. Actually, what I want to talk about here is just one of these ads: John Helmer's for European Berets.

The ad, which features a small postage-stamp sized photo of Mr. Helmer wearing one of his berets and an expression of what I guess you might call wistful delight, has been a perpetual and unexpected source of fascination to me for years now. The reasons are many. For one thing, the brick-and-mortar establishment behind it is not located in some distant, incomprehensible place like Hopkinton, Massachusetts, or Sleepy Hollow, New York, but right here in Portland, Oregon. For another, it seems—from an accountancy point of view—so proudly and resolutely irresponsible. It makes no economic sense. Whatever the glossies gloss, it doesn't seem likely that anyone—not even the cock-eyed-est of optimists—could possibly have believed that this is an investment that would pay for itself. (A casual calculation based on the current ad rates for just one of the magazines suggests they would have to sell at least 15 of these berets a day just to break even.)

If this little ad does not—cannot—pay for itself, why do the people in charge at Helmer's continue to run it? I don't know, but I have a theory that I have been very careful not to test—namely, that this is not your standard shopkeeper's gambit, but an act of charity that the proprietor, the man behind it, the man whose name is on the door, is one of those rarest of creatures: a businessman with broadened interests; a man with Enlightenment values; a man who believes in the idea of an educated public, in the "emancipation of human consciousness," in the elevating effects of a high-dose exposure to art; a man willing to sacrifice a certain amount of personal gain for a greater, less grasping good.

Because Helmer's supports *Harper's* and *The New Yorker*, I support Helmer's—though not nearly as well as I would like. In part this is because of their inventory, which is classic and fairly formal, and my taste in clothes, which is classic but distinctly informal. I have over the years bought gloves, sweaters, two or three coats, and I don't know how many umbrellas from them. Established in 1921 and identifying itself as a "Haberdashery," the place is best known around town as simply "the hat store." I don't wear hats that often myself—I have an oddly shaped head and look like an idiot in one—but I have bought at least a half dozen for my father-in-law who is getting a little thin on top.

In supporting these magazines Helmer's is supporting the writers who appear in them, writers I admire like Gary Shteyngart, Nicole Krauss, and Rivka Galchen. Helmer's is putting actual money in these writers' pockets, which means, by extension, so am I. Penciled out it isn't much of a contribution, of course—an infinitesimal, barely calculable, fraction of what is already a proportionally miniscule amount— but it is a contribution nonetheless. (Occasionally I like to distract myself—like when I am waiting for an oil change—by imaginatively following this minuscule contribution of mine. I like to think that in buying a new raincoat I have helped put some gas in Jonathan Franzen's car, some milk in Jeffrey Eugenides's refrigerator, some batteries in Alice Munro's flashlight. I like to think I have helped Rick Moody hire a plumber and that I have chipped in on that cup of coffee that kept the late David Foster Wallace awake that Wednesday night when he was holed up in his bat-cave researching the evolutionary history of crustaceans for his Lobster Festival essay.)

Mr. Helmer's shop and sometimes his ad have made both planned and unplanned appearances in several of my novels—usually in what the professors would call an objective correlative–ish role, as a sort of stand-in, a piece of subliminal commentary. It has also made planned and unplanned appearances in my photographic work, and I would not be surprised to see it making additional appearances in photographs yet to come. The hat, by virtue of its privileged perch, occupies a special place in fashion's vocabulary. It is the final piece of the sartorial puzzle, the concluding point in a comment on identity. I am fascinated with them for this reason. I am also fascinated with them because of the aforementioned affliction—the inability to wear one well myself. Somewhere in almost every picture I take that involves a hat, there is, I think, a little bit of envy.

In his book *The Ongoing Moment* (a stream-of-consciousness amble through the history of photography), Geoff Dyer takes up the subject of the hat—a thing he sees as closely associated with the documentary photography of the 1930s. The hat, which had been essentially a status identifier, was transformed by a decimating depression into an existential emblem of hardship and despair—especially as it appeared in the work of Dorothea Lang and Walker Evans. "By the 1950s," however, Dyer writes, "the great era of the hat in photography had passed. Wearing a hat was optional where once it had been almost obligatory, and it was no longer a reliable indicator of the ravages inflicted on men by economic forces beyond their control or understanding. The hat became just a hat." This is not a sentiment I have a lot of sympathy for. Sometimes perhaps a hat is just a hat—just as Freud said, sometimes a cigar is just a cigar—but most often it is something more. Some are weighed down with more meaning than others, of course, but they are all to one degree or another symbolic things. Sometimes their significations are clear and simple, but more often they are not—they are complex, encrypted, obscure. Properly decoded, they are invariably clues to character. If one era of the hat in photography passed in the 1950s when the hat ceased to be an obligatory accoutrement, a new era began when it became an object of choice. In the 1960s it re-emerged as a character and/or cultural indicator, and it continues as such today. This new era of the hat in photography is a subject worthy of critical attention—both the streamlined sort and the scholarly. I am sure the current Mr. Helmer would agree.

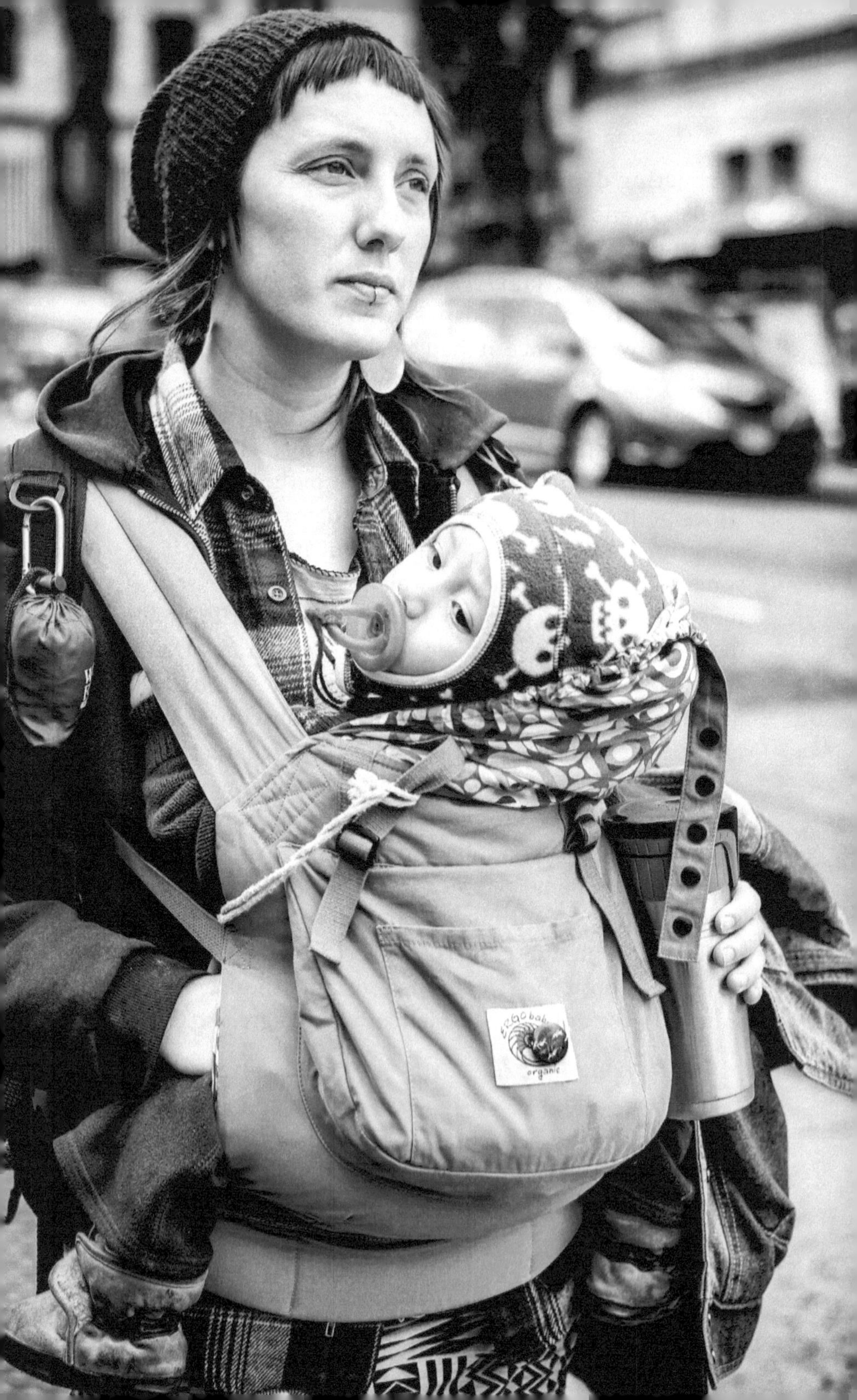

A VISIBLE VIVIAN

Excerpts from a Journal

I AM NOT THE SORT OF PERSON WHO IS INCLINED TO WRITE fan letters, but this morning I found myself unexpectedly tempted to send off some sort of effusive note to a photographer by the name of Vivian Maier. I did in the end resist the temptation, however, as Ms. Maier is dead and I simply could not imagine her caring one way or the other about my opinion of her work. Eccentric and secretive, she was a Chicago nanny by day and a street photographer extraordinaire by night. A young man named John Maloof—who bought tens of thousands of her negatives at a flea-market sale—posted a handful of her photographs online. It is remarkable work, and I am eager to see more. The accessibility of it will be a problem at some point, I suspect, as "accessibility" seems to be viewed these days the way

Photo: Mother and Child, 2013

"consistency" was once famously viewed by the ethereal Mr. Emerson—that is, as the hobgoblin of little minds.

—

Saw a short television report about John Maloof's miraculous discovery of reclusive nanny-photographer Vivian Maier. The host of the show was one of those slim, fastidious sorts. He reminded me somehow of a dentist—not just any dentist, but the sort who would subject you to unnecessary procedures (extractions, crowns, bridges) for the sake of his dimpled daughter's college fund.

Maloof himself seemed boyish and sincere, but there is something about him that bothers me. The genuineness of his sincerity perhaps? I am not sure he is someone I would trust. It is not just that he has cornered the market on Ms. Maier's negatives, but that he has started to gather up ephemera—her hats, her cameras, her shoes, boxes of her clothes. He is a twenty-seven year old garage-sale treasure-hunter who has apparently hit it big. He is the man who is now editing and exhibiting Ms. Maier's work—the man who is speaking for her. He may have some sort of legal right, but I wonder if he has a moral one. What idea do you suppose he has of Ms. Maier's aesthetic sensibilities or her intentions?

And the Baylaenders—for whom Vivian once worked—what can I say about them? They were interviewed for the piece. Mrs. Baylaender (in her gold necklace and phosphorescent sweater) chose to spend her few minutes on national television quietly defaming her former nanny—passing on complaints about Ms. Maier's manners and an anonymous reference to her as "that awful lady." Ms. Maier may have been an awful lady—I don't know. After seeing this, however, I wouldn't be surprised to find someone out there right now willing to say this very thing about Mrs. Baylaender.

—

Read an article today in *Chicago Magazine* by Nora O'Donnell. She did a very nice job of outlining what has become "the Vivian Maier story." (Mysterious Chicago nanny discovered after death to be world-class street photographer.) She referred to John Maloof as a "third-generation reseller." I don't know exactly what that is, but I can tell you the title does not gives me any comfort. She describes in detail his purchasing the negatives repossessed from Maier's storage locker and discovering via the internet a wide-spread interest in the work. I suspect the picture O'Donnell has given of Vivian will color much of whatever there is to come—for instance, that she was proudly a "Miss" and not a "Mrs."

In addition to interviewing a number of Vivian's former employers, O'Donnell interviewed Colin Westerbeck, the former curator of photography at the Art Institute of Chicago. He offered up a classic example of curatorial cowardliness with an empty reference to Ms. Maier as an "interesting case." One moment he is saying she lacks the irony and wit of her Chicago contemporaries, the next that she captures the character of the city and works the streets in a "savvy" way. I think I'll start referring to weasels as westerbecks. His concern is not with Maier's work, but with his status as a sophisticate. He is not going to wander out onto the peer-reviewed savannah in a pair of pork-chop pants—that is, formulate a real opinion without credentialed back-up.

—

Just read Aaron Sigmond's article in *American Photo*: "Vivian Maier, Invisible Woman." I can only imagine that at this moment Ms. Maier wishes she were invisible. I suspect she wishes it more with each passing day.

It is both amusing and annoying to see Maloof's cache of Ms. Maier's negatives referred to now as the "Maloof Collection" and to hear that he has recently acquired a "communications adviser"—someone named Martin Fuchs. "It's important to us," Fuchs says, "that we do the right thing: establish Vivian Maier as the great photographer she was and get her work seen and known." Of course, it is also important to their bank accounts.

If nothing else good comes from this particular article, at least the Gensburgs have gotten a few kind words. Ms. Maier worked for them for 17 years and was apparently a sort of second mother to John, Lane, and Matthew. They are remarkable people, the sort everyone wishes they knew—people with large hearts. They stayed in touch with Ms. Maier long after she left them. They helped her with an apartment and a nursing home in those last years and in the end scattered her ashes in the North Shore woods where they used to pick strawberries. (A romantic gesture certainly, but one I suspect Ms. Maier might still have appreciated.)

—

Read Alex Kotlowitz's article in *Mother Jones*. The Maier story it seems is still new and exciting—eccentric nanny, secret world-class photographer, John Maloof, storage box of photographic negatives, $400, etc., etc. I noticed in the article that Mr. Maloof has stopped referring to himself as "a third-generation flea market seller." He now refers to himself as a real-estate agent and historian. He has tracked down additional boxes of Ms. Maier's negatives. He now owns more than 100,000 of them.

Kotlowitz did a nice job of capturing the basic impulse of Ms. Maier's work, which is quintessentially democratic. There are photographs of rich and poor, young and old, black and white, people having a good time, and people not having a good time. He quotes the cloying Joel Meyerowitz, street photography's reigning potentate, saying she was a humanist and you could find that everywhere in her photographs.

—

Read David Zax's short piece in the *Smithsonian Magazine*. Yet another mention of Ms. Maier's "sturdy shoes" or, in this case, "boots"—winking code for a certain sexual orientation. Ink and innuendo—they are the life-blood of freelance journalism.

Zax mentions another collector—someone named Jeffrey Goldstein. Apparently he has scooped up what the omnivorous John Maloof has missed—another 15,000 negatives.

—

Bought a copy of Maloof's book that just came out: *Vivian Maier, Street Photographer*. It is hard to know where to start. Maloof says that from the beginning he has been seeking to preserve Vivian's legacy the "right" way. I have a feeling that in a mercantile sense this is true, but that he is not quite the hero he wants us to believe he is. He tells us what he has done is essentially save Vivian from herself—that the disposition of her work was endangered by her "intense" sense of privacy. He says she lacked confidence in her work. I suspect he thinks this assertion justifies his predation in some way. While I like many of the photographs he has chosen here, I can't help but feel there has been a rush to publication. The editing is iffy, and the print quality is not what it should be.

—

There is one thing you find in Ms. Maier's work that you do not find in most other street photographer's (Garry Winogrand, for instance): empathy. It is part of what attracts the general public to her and part of what repels the toffee-nosed professoriate. Empathetic work is immediately suspect by its very nature —a middlebrow tell. It reminds me of the complaints lodged against Andre Kertez—that his work was too humanistic, not ironic or edgy enough.

—

Bought a new book by Richard Cahan and Michael Williams—*Vivian Maier: Out of the Shadows*. The images are from the Jeffrey Goldstein collection. I don't know what to make of him—Mr. Goldstein. It is, in part, the facial hair. One moment he is modeling a goatee, the next a "soul patch." Looks demonic. But in some sense everyone involved in this enterprise has started to look demonic to me. Goldstein seems a different sort of opportunist from Mr. Maloof—perhaps more artistically motivated. He was a cabinetmaker. Still, trepidatious. Uncomfortable.

As for the book—it feels better than Maloof's. It is the right size, heavy, well-printed. There are some good photographs here, but there are a number that should not have been included. I suspect this was not just a matter of taste, but of inventory. Mr. Goldstein has fewer images than Maloof to choose from.

—

Rummaging around in *Out of the Shadows*. Tempted to

start listing the photographs I found particularly good, but I won't. I couldn't mention this one without mentioning that one or that one without mentioning this other one, etc., etc. Such a list gets ridiculous before you know it. I would say in general that I have a weakness for the downtown stuff and that I do not share Ms. Maier's interest in children or the beach.

—

Saw the Maloof documentary yesterday: *Finding Vivian Maier*. I have mixed feelings about it. On one hand I got a firmer sense of Ms. Maier—certainly a firmer sense than she would have liked. On the other, I got a firmer sense of Mr. Maloof. He spent the first half of the film showing us what a dogged detective he was—amassing not just information, but trophies. In one especially tasteless scene he spreads a large cache of Ms. Maier's belongings out in neat piles across the floor—hats, blouses, and old bus passes. The point was ostensibly to show us how much there was, to allude to Ms. Maier's hoarding issues, but I had the distinct feeling that what I was looking at was not evidence of neurosis, but a future tax deduction. If things go well for Mr. Maloof, each of these items will one day have a nice little price tag attached to them.

As for the thing as a whole, it was a bit darker than I expected. Largely because one important piece was missing—the Genzbergs, the family Vivian lived with longest and who knew her best.

The interviews were a tangle of ambiguous and

contradictory accounts. Everyone, it seemed, had a complaint or an unflattering recollection. No assertion was challenged. No effort was made to verify any claim. One family, the Matthews, went out of their way to cast a shadow over Vivian's memory. They described her as mentally ill and as a likely victim of molestation. Also included (for tabloid reasons?) was a completely bizarre story from Inger Raymond—an obese woman with obvious problems who claimed Ms. Maier used to force-feed her.

Read a review of Maloof's documentary by Malcolm Jones. He describes it as "fascinating but ultimately troubling." I agree completely. A few of the things he lists as troubling, however, are not so troubling to me— for example, Maloof portraying himself as the sole discoverer of Ms. Maier's work when we know from previous reporting that there were several other people involved. The issue of editorial control, however, is another matter. That is very troubling.

Read a piece in *The New Yorker* by Rose Lichter-Marck titled *Vivian Maier and the Problem of Difficult Women*. It is a not particularly well-put-together feministic complaint. Ms. Lichter-Marck sees an insult to women in the general reaction to Ms. Maier's story—a suggestion that domestic work (women's work) is seen as somehow incompatible with artistic ambition. I agree and disagree. There is obviously bias, but I don't think it is so much a gender bias as it is a class or status bias. There would be a similar sort of suggestion if the work in question had been blue-collar (men's work). A longshoreman who wrote philosophical treatises, for instance. (See Eric Hoffer.) She says the "stories of difficult women can be unflattering even when they are told in praise," suggesting blatantly and wrongly that the same is not true of stories told about difficult men. (See any Jackson Pollock biography.) She says "the unconventional choices of women are explained in the language of mental illness…as symptoms of pathology rather than as an active response to structural challenges or mere preference," suggesting blatantly, wrongly, and awkwardly that the same is not true of the unconventional choices of men. (Again, see any Jackson Pollock biography.) She says a male with Vivian's particular set of peculiarities would be treated very differently. I don't think that is true. If we took Ms. Maier's story and changed only two things—gender and occupation (secretive, unmarried, idiosyncratic auto mechanic discovered after death to be world-class street photographer)—we would have been equally as fascinated. It would be ridiculous to deny there is some gender bias involved in all of this, but I don't think it is the foreground issue that Ms. Lichter-Marck does.

———

I see where Ron Slattery—one of the earliest raiders of the lost storage lockers—is suing a gallery that was selling some of the original Maier prints that he had. He is claiming these prints were damaged by the gallery and that the gallery tried to cover this up. Why do I have the feeling this is not going to be the last story about Ms. Maier's archive featuring a lawyer?

Maloof's documentary was just released in England. It seems to be causing a bit of a controversy. No need to worry though—there is a new academic on the case: Pamela Bannos. She is a professor of photography in Northwestern University's Department of Art Theory and Practice. I know nothing about her except that she seems preternaturally persistent—a quality that is never easy to decode.

I knew we would eventually be getting around to the lawyers. There is a court case now in Chicago that could bring the Vivian Maier juggernaut—exhibitions, books, lectures, movies, prints—to a halt for years. A lawyer by the name of David Deal (how appropriate) says he has tracked down an heir to the estate—a cousin once-removed.

—

Saw an article in *The Reader* today with a wonderful title: "Losing Vivian Maier." The synopsis was equally wonderful: "John Maloof and Jeffrey Goldstein turned their caches of negatives by the late street photographer and 'North Shore nanny' into full-time jobs. Now the government wants in." In short, more lawyers.

Deal's filing apparently inspired the Cook County Probate Court. They wrote a letter to everyone involved with the Maier estate telling them to hold onto their records as there might be copyright issues.

—

Apparently the David Deal lawsuit has inspired Mr. Goldstein to call a halt to his exploitation of Ms. Maier's archive. He has sold his 17,500 negatives to the Stephen Bulger Gallery in Toronto. He will not say for how much—it would ruin the narrative, the one where he isn't in it for the money. He can't tell us, he says, what pain it caused him to do this. He is consoled now only by his bank balance.

—

It seems there is now a new investigator at work—a woman named Ann Marks. She describes herself as a retired business woman who likes to look things up.

Apparently she, like Bannos, has turned up some information on Vivian's long-missing brother, Charles.

—

I have to admit, if not for Mr. Maloof neither I nor anyone else might have come across this remarkable work of Ms. Maier. The fact that his first motive was to make a buck makes me suspicious of all his following acclamations of reverence. I think he has come to appreciate the work in some way, but is still just basically trying to add value to his holdings. He has done a lot of work. He wants to get paid. He should get paid. But how much and in what manner? Not as much as I think he would like and not in the manner I think he would like. A small royalty, I think, would be ethically sufficient.

—

Read Jason Meisner's article in the *Chicago Tribune*. It is all about the legal battle to determine who has the right to produce and to sell Ms. Maier's work. They are saying the collection could be worth millions of dollars. The new information about the long-lost brother, Charles, comes from the woman I mentioned earlier: Ann Marks. She says Charles worked as a music teacher, served in the Army, and died nearly four decades ago in a small town in central New Jersey. The question no one seems to be able to answer yet is "did he have children"—that is, heirs. In addition to all of the amateur sleuths, there is a cadre of expensive geneologists who have been hired to look into this. Everyone wants to find someone somewhere so they can settle the copyright issues and get back to making money.

Marks says Charles was a drug addict, had run-ins with the law, was dishonorably discharged from the Army, and was diagnosed with schizophrenia. According to mysterious "documents and letters" she has concluded there was alcoholism in the family and that the marriage of Ms. Maier's parents was unhappy. They have found (or constructed) exactly what they have been looking for: divorce, alcoholism, mental illness. If only they could find a murderer—that would be a narrative nugget that was worth a few dollars.

I see in the *Tribune* that a deal with Cook County is in the works, but everyone is staying quiet about it. There are still some negotiations going on. I would wish a plague on all their houses, but I would like the archive opened and set free so we could see more of Ms. Maier's engaging work. Let us hope.

Bought Pamela Bannos's new biography, *Vivian Maier: A Photographer's Life and Afterlife*. She says her book is a "counterpoint, a counternarrative, and a corrective to the public depiction of Vivian Maier and her work." I want to be on her side, but she makes it difficult. It is obvious from the beginning, from the "Introduction," that the narrative to follow will be as biased in its own way as the one it seeks to counter.

Three-quarters of the way through the Bannos book. For all of its virtues, it has some serious structural problems. Two stories—one of Ms. Maier's life, the other of her archive's life—are woven together with a thumbnail history of street photography that feels a lot like stuffing. The idea, I think, was to break up some of the duller bits—the swing through the family tree, the history of eBay transactions, the outline of copyright law—to create some sort of drama or suspense, but the insistent, haphazard flipping back and forth from one story to the other does nothing but annoy. It drains much of the life from the book.

The structure is not the book's only problem, however: there is the overwhelming meticulousness of the research. Thoroughness is welcome—it illuminates, contextualizes, establishes authority up to a point. You know when Ms. Bannos writes "Vivian Dorothy Maier was born in New York City on February 1, 1926, a cold and rainy Monday" that she has consulted not only the relevant birth records, but the meteorological ones as well. I admire this sort of hyper-assiduity, but—as the line between conscientious academic and obsessive/compulsive blurs—it can feel a little creepy, a little stalkeresque. Bannos has put an extraordinary amount of time and effort into this project. She cannot help but want to empty her notebooks, to show her work. There is a place, however, where detail no longer serves the subject, where a data dump obscures as much as it reveals.

⌒

Finished the Bannos book. It will be, I suspect, the primary source of information on all things Vivian Maier for quite some time. Ms. Bannos describes her subject as a woman with a difficult personality who chose to remain unknown. She does not see her invasion of Ms. Maier's privacy as being in any way the equivalent of Mr. Maloof's. She shields herself with a steely belief in the purity of her motives. What happens, I wonder, to the money Ms. Bannos makes on this book? Does it go into her bank account or into some virtuous nonprofit enterprise? What about speaking fees, consultancies, etc., etc.?

I thank Ms. Bannos for this book, but I can't imagine Ms. Maier would.

Photo: Annex Bar, 2014

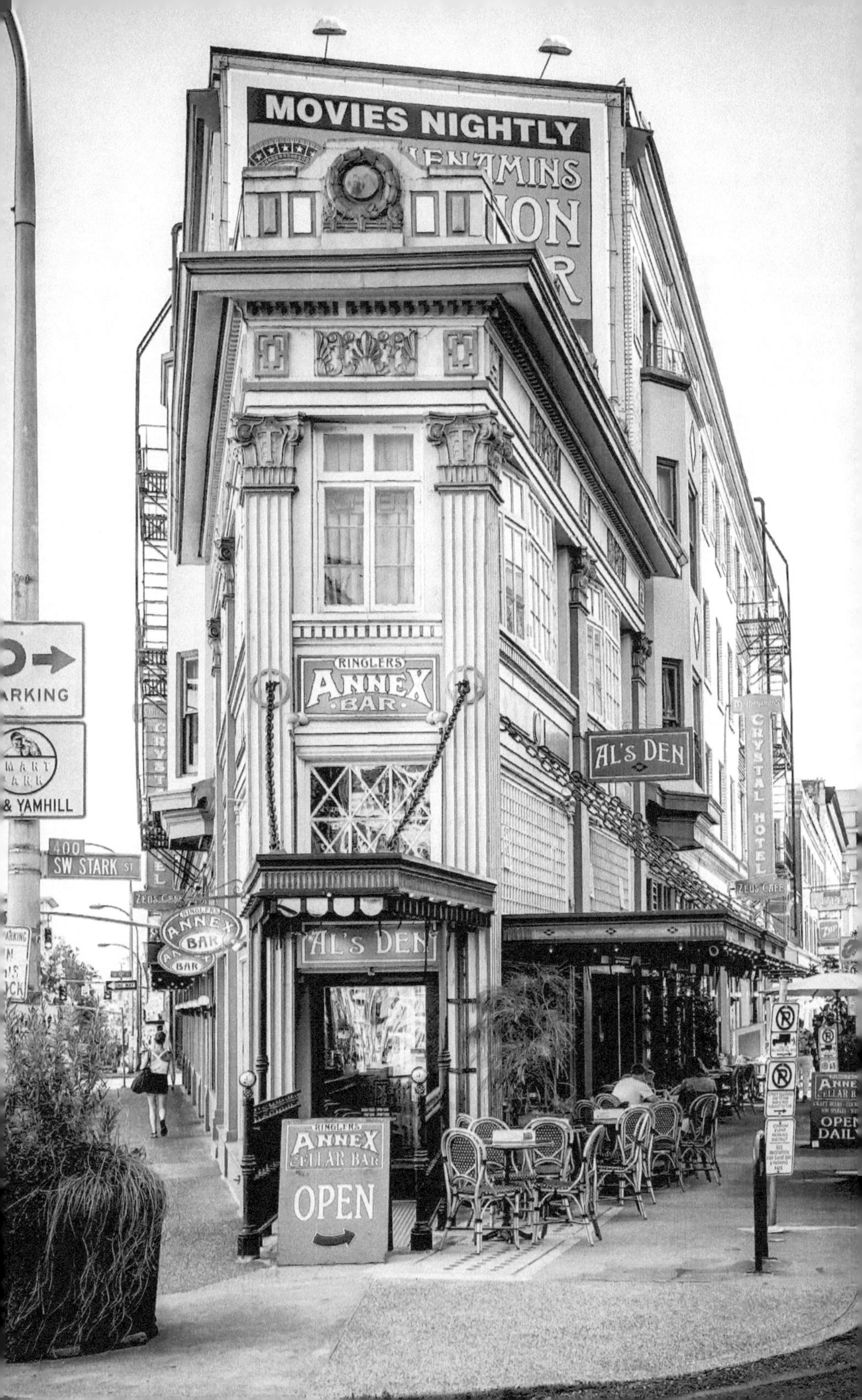

MOVIES NIGHTLY
MENAMINS
NON
AR
RINGLERS
ANNEX
BAR
AL'S DEN
CRYSTAL HOTEL
ZEUS CAFE
ANNEX
BAR
AL'S DEN
RINGLERS
ANNEX
CELLAR BAR
OPEN
PARKING
& YAMHILL
400
SW STARK ST
RINGLERS
ANNEX
CELLAR BAR
OPEN
DAILY

THE CRITIC'S EYE

Janet Malcolm's *Diana & Nikon* is rightly considered by many to be one of photography's canonical texts. A collection of essays written over a number of years in response to various occasions (photography exhibitions, the publication of photography books), it offers a remarkably lucid and enduring survey of its maddeningly enigmatic subject.

In her preface to the original edition of the book, Malcolm demurs. She says it took her a long time to get a handle on the medium; that she was midway into the book before she felt she had got hold of the subject; and that it was not until the ninth essay, "Two Roads, One Destination," that she began to "untangle some of [photography's] knottier issues." This is, of course, Malcolm simply being Malcolmly-modest. She had a handle on the subject from the beginning—from the opening essay "East and West" in which she reviewed a pair of biographies, one of Alfred Stieglitz that offered a brave, if not entirely exculpatory, defense of the reflexively maligned Photo-Secessionist movement (it introduced formalism into photography) and the other of Edward Weston in which she dissected the photographer's curious oeuvre before wandering off into the weeds of his very weedy domestic life as all writers on Weston inevitably must—his wives, his many lovers, his sad end (Parkinson's and thirty cats).

The essay Malcolm singles out by name in her preface, "Two Roads, One Destination," is important primarily for the introduction in which she divides the complex world of photography into polarized camps with a revelatory analogy.

The essay opens with a lengthy epigraph from the famously pugnacious critic Clement Greenberg who wrote: "The limitations that constitute the medium of painting—the flat surface, the shape of the support, the properties of pigment—were treated by the Old Masters as negative factors that could be acknowledged only implicitly or indirectly. Modernist painting has come to regard these same limitations as positive factors that are to be acknowledged openly. Manet's paintings became the first modernist ones by virtue of the frankness with which they declared the surfaces on which they were painted."

The relationship of photography to painting is one of Malcolm's frequent topics—a central interest to her, to other critics, and to photographers forty years ago when this essay was originally written. "Photography went modernist not, as has been supposed, when it began to imitate modern abstract art but when it began to study snapshots." Robert Frank, "the Manet of the New Photography," embraced what previous generations of art photographers had sought to conceal—the artless chaos at the heart of the medium as represented by the amateur or vernacular photograph. He "shed all the pictorial values of his predecessors—composition, design, tonal balance, print quality—and produced pictures that look as if a kid had taken them." He showed photography, Malcolm says, "at its most nakedly photographic."

From this quick, prescient, crystalline critique (smudged slightly by a strained, but not entirely outlandish, association of New Photography with Action Painting), Malcolm transitioned to the job at hand—reviewing two exhibitions: one by avant-gardist Eve Sonneman and the other by famous formalist Harry Callahan. "As each side digs out its position—the avant-garde going deeper and deeper into its examination of the photographic, the old guard into the making of medium-transcending beautiful forms—the gap between them seems to be *narrowing* [italics hers] rather than widening." This is, I'm afraid, a creaky contention. It is true that many in these camps do not seem wholly one thing or the other—convention-ignoring modernists, rule-constricted traditionalists—but the idea that somehow this has not always been the case and is, in fact, evidence of some sort of trend is mostly, I think, a trope of convenience. It is Malcolm setting the table not just for her reviews of Sonneman and Callahan, but for an argument in conclusion that some might find unflatteringly retrograde.

Malcolm is a generous, no-nonsense sort of writer with a journalist's inclination to be open-minded, but you can feel her struggling with both of these exhibitions—more maybe with Sonneman (where she lapses into art-speak and Duchamp references) than with Callahan (where she gets a little help from a high-flying friend, John Szarkowski, Director of the Department of Photography at The Museum of Modern Art). Neither offers an ideal example of the points she wants to make.

The photographs in the Sonneman exhibition are shown in framed pairs. Each set offers a slightly different to drastically different view of the same subject. The idea, as Malcolm reports, is to challenge a "core concept; namely, that there is such a thing as *the* picture of something." With these pairings, Malcolm writes, "Sonneman argues that there is only *a* picture—that any photograph taken is inevitably arbitrary." This idea—which I suspect wafts up from the artist's statement—sounds good if you don't think about it, but is it in any way illuminative? Isn't this just semantical footsie? What image isn't "inevitably arbitrary"?

This is needy work—it comes with a supplicating demand for interpretation. "Singly, Sonneman's pictures are without interest," Malcolm writes. "Conjointly, they are respectable works of avant-garde art." They contain "an aesthetic residue." Perhaps, but one would need an unusually sensitive sort of spectrograph to detect it. The work may offer a "critique of photography," but it offers little visual interest—grist for the critic's quill, but little or nothing for the hapless viewer.

The second exhibition Malcolm reviews is a collection of Harry Callahan's work at the Light Gallery. "Callahan has produced some of the purest and most austere abstract photography in our time," Malcolm says. "His career is one of those monuments to dedication and work and care and belief in self that command respect even where they do not induce love."

Callahan is, Malcolm suggests, an old-fashioned photographer—one often mistaken for a Modernist. His work is connected to the painterly tradition of photography. It is "stylistically of a piece, marked by a kind of exquisite dryness, a quietness and evenness of tone, and a quality of muted restraint, almost grudgingness." It is hard to respond to, she says, "the way a quiet, drab-looking person at a party is hard to go up and talk to." But it is Malcolm's job to respond to it, and respond she does.

The show (photographs of frame houses in Providence) was uncharacteristically in color. Malcolm finds it was "this 'vulgar' touch, this concession to the childish (human) craving for pleasure, that broke down [her] resistance to Callahan and permitted [her] to experience one of those rare moments of aesthetic joy...that arrive when one is suddenly able to appreciate, understand, and enjoy what has hitherto been thwarting, boring, off-putting." For me this revelatory moment feels suspiciously self-induced. Mark Twain once boasted of his memory, saying he could remember a thing whether it happened or not. It is easy, I think, for a critic on a mission to feel a thing whether it is there to be felt or not.

Malcolm sees in Callahan "the greatness that [she] once merely accepted other people's word for," and in a key passage she gives us a glimpse of the point she has been wanting to make from the beginning: photographs "are not less truthful because the photographer has sought to make them beautiful; they express the more comprehensive, if not higher, truth of art. It is the absence of this kind of ordering that makes itself felt in the work of avant-garde photographers...and that makes so much of their realism look like triviality." She is comfortable giving snap-shooters their due, but she wants to make the case that their recent ascendance has not invalidated more considered work.

She returns to this point sixteen years later in a beautiful essay on the photographer Sally Mann that appears in the second edition of *Diana & Nikon*: "During John Szarkowski's tenure as director of photography at the Modern he cultivated a kind of photography that Sally Mann brings to triumphant, sometimes transcendent, fruition." He "distinguished between the calculated, well-made... art photograph and the artless but vitally interesting snapshot, and he supported photographers who attempted the *tour de force* of art snapshot." The photographers he championed, however, "put greater pressure on the snapshot side of the equation; their pictures are looser, messier, 'uglier'.... In Sally Mann's photographs the scale tips back toward the older 'beautiful' photograph—without, however, any diminution of the appearance of photojournalistic chanciness." It seems clear where

Malcolm's sympathies lay. She is careful. She knows the arguments for mediation can be easily characterized as reactionary.

———

In her conclusion Malcolm loops back around to an exhibition of Stieglitz's photography collection that she had seen the previous summer at the Metropolitan Museum and to yet another not-fully-fathomable defense of the Photo-Secessionists. The argument is essentially that "yes" they may have been up to no good (they fiddled with their photographs for painterly effects), but they were better than what went before—the "ludicrously anecdotal art photographs" of Oscar Rejlander, for example. The Secessionist's work referenced better painters (Pre-Raphaelites, Impressionists), and they were strong on design. This was, Malcolm suggests in one of the essay's most strained assertions, an indication of "their involvement with photography's processes" and "foreshadowed the modernism of Frank by a good fifty years." Yes, and one could say the Lasxvux cave painting foreshadowed the modernism of Frank by a good five thousand years. That would be equally true.

This essay was in many ways an answer to her earlier essay, "Diana and Nikon," the essay that gave this book its name. It was published in 1976 when a gallon of gas cost .59 cents and Gerald Ford was President. It was a brief look at the state of the medium, a heebie-jeebies inducing analysis of the "malaise" that Malcolm found hanging over what was then contemporary photography.

It opened with a review of John Szarkowski's *The Photographer's Eye*—a work that Malcolm saw as the critical equivalent of Mrs. O'Leary's cow, kicking over certain assumptions about the nature of photography and inadvertently burning down the house. Szarkowski, esteemed Director of MOMA and godfather of the snapshot aesthetic, wanted to look at "photography" as a whole—he wanted to see what united the medium's various genres: art photography, photojournalism, commercial photography, and an "increasingly ubiquitous" amateur photography. Removing individual samples of these works from their contexts, he sorted them according to a set of essential criteria: "The Thing Itself," "The Detail," "The Frame," "Time," and "Vantage Point"—what he took to be the inherent properties of all photographs. "A surprising and disturbing impression [emerged] from this mélange of artistic and non-artistic photographs," Malcolm writes. "One would [have expected] the artless pictures to suffer when compared to the conscious works of art that surrounded them, but, oddly enough, they [did] not."

Thumbing through the book was, Malcolm says, "a shattering experience" for those who supported the claim of photography as an art form. The idea that "in the hands of a great talent" photography could "ascend to the level of art [was] overturned by Szarkowski's anthology" starting a widespread status panic.

It may be, Malcolm glumly mused, that the golden age of photography created by the likes of Stieglitz, Weston, Strand, Cartier-Bresson, and Kertesz was "a single aberrant episode in the medium whose truest purposes are fulfilled not by artists...but by artisans and amateurs."

The relationship of photography to painting is a long and complex one. It is, as I mentioned earlier, a central issue for Malcolm. Her essays are decorated with painters' names—Picasso, Kline, deKooning, Mondrian, Hopper, O'Keefe, Whistler, Bacon, Rivera, Rembrandt, Degas, etc., etc. Her focus on this relationship should be considered in context. The protective inclination to tie photography to painting has not disappeared, but it is not what it used to be. Now that photography's struggle for acceptance as a legitimate art form has largely been won, there is no longer a need for these sorts of nervous justifications.

From the beginning photographers have been asking themselves about the nature of their mysterious medium—its "form," Malcolm writes, is an "inherent preoccupation." This is true. That this native concern creates a special relationship to modernism that took "form" as one of its central subjects is also true, but only in the broadest sense—broad to the point of being meaningless.

"The apparent differences between today's photographic avant-garde and the old guard are not as great as the hidden affinities," Malcolm writes. Another questionable contention. These two camps "arrive at different conclusions about the nature of photography, but they ask the same questions, and questions are what matter, of course." Yes, the questions matter, but not more than the conclusions. This is more a facile exit from the essay than a working thesis. The fact that contemporary work—both old-guardish and avant-gardish—"calls attention to art" is not enough to join these contending factions in holy matrimony. It is not a destination—it is an intersection.

Together the essays in this collection offer a smart tour of the medium. While Malcolm has written brilliantly about Victorian literature, psychiatry, and murder, her passionate interest in the visual arts has never abated. There is, for instance, the relatively recent essay titled "Depth of Field" (written thirty-five years after *Diana*) about German photographer Thomas Struth, master of the monster print. It is what you would expect: candid, lucid, adventurous—a work of steely resolve advocating, as always, for the "comprehensive, if not higher, truth of art."

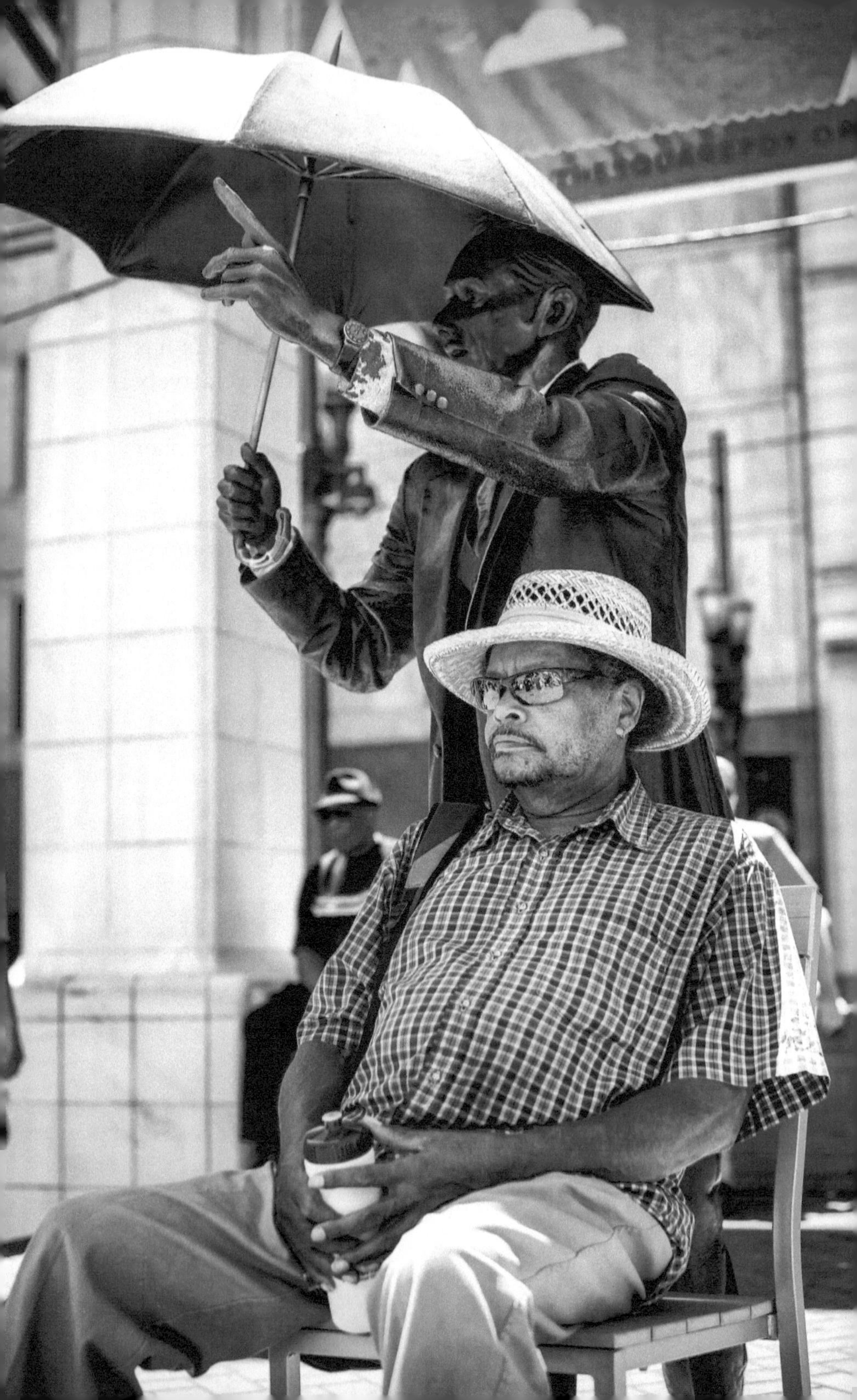

THE PHOTOGRAPHIC JOURNAL

The images included in my latest book of photographs were excerpted from a larger ongoing project—from what is basically a photographic journal, a personalized and idiosyncratic survey of the world around me, an archive that serves in its own special way as a species of memoir. My hope was, as always, to document—to capture and to preserve for myself and others a transient moment of aesthetic pleasure, a strong sense of the subject, a resonating mix of common and individual experience. A storehouse of meanings and mysteries, it is an archive that shares in many ways the characteristics of a written work.

Joan Didion—the novelist, essayist, and screenwriter—wrote a piece many years ago on the subject of keeping a journal. Wandering aimlessly through a

Photo: Umbrella Man, 2013

set of her cryptic notes from years before, she found herself periodically perplexed by various entries. She found herself wondering why she had chosen to write this or that particular thing down—just as I, wandering aimlessly through my photographic archive, find myself periodically wondering why I decided to take this or that photograph. The keepers of notebooks are, Didion says, "anxious malcontents, children afflicted apparently at birth with some presentiment of loss." So too are many photographers. "The impulse to preserve lies at the bottom of all art," wrote the poet Phillip Larkin. It certainly lies at the heart of the documentary impulse.

"The point of keeping a notebook has never been… to have an accurate factual record." Didion writes. This is where our paths diverge as "journalists." The photographic urge as opposed to the calligraphic is born of what Didion calls an "instinct for reality"—an instinct she sometimes honors, but as a card-carrying Romantic usually disparages. "I always had trouble distinguishing between what happened and what merely might have happened, but I remain unconvinced that the distinction, for my purposes, matters," she said. For the photographer's purposes the distinction matters a great deal. For Didion it is the unfettered imagination vs. a cretinous literalism—a gross and self-aggrandizing simplification. Good old everyday rise-and-shine "reality" is the fundamental subject of photography. It may seem mundane, but it is essentially miraculous. If nothing else, it possesses what James Agee once called "the cruel radiance of what is."

For Didion it is the embroidered bit of fiction that

brings a past event to life—for the photographer it is the simple (if inevitably inflected) statement of fact. Facts are food for the imagination. "How it felt to me:" Didion says, "that is...the truth about a notebook." How it was to be: that is the truth about a photographic journal. The powers of imagination work one way, the powers of observation another. Working in tandem, you get an artist.

Our paths converge again—Ms. Didion's and mine—when you look at the uses we have made of our respective journals. The products of an "inexplicable compulsion," they are aides to memory and sources of inspiration. Individual entries—a note, a photograph—may puzzle from time to time, but studied carefully they almost always reveal their meanings.

There is no greater instrument for the exploration of experience (both real and imagined) than the written word, but the language we use is not the only one available to us. Photography is another language—like music. Each has its own rhetoric, its own eloquence— one silver-tongued, the other silver-gelatin tongued. One is weighted with subjective truths, the other with objective, but each is invariably a complex mixture of both. Each type of journal—the written and photographic—is an arcane accumulation of experience. Each is accessed and processed differently, but both are the progeny of magic.

These journals—written and photographic—are warehouses of information, and embedded in that information like raisins in an oatmeal cookie are clues to the people behind them, clues to who he or she was in both the near and distant past. Keeping in touch with that person—the person one was—"is what a notebook is all about," Didion writes. It might not be quite what a photographic journal is all about, but it is certainly part of it. Keeping in touch with who you were is the first step to understanding both who you are and who you may one day want to be.

In the written journal "the common denominator… is always…the implacable 'I'," Didion says. Its focus is almost always on one's own life. In all but the most solipsistic of photographic journals the focus tends to be on life in a more general sense. Each sort of journal is, in the end, a unique form of communion with the world, a singular and distinctive effort to know.

———

Photo: Girl with Cigarette, 2017

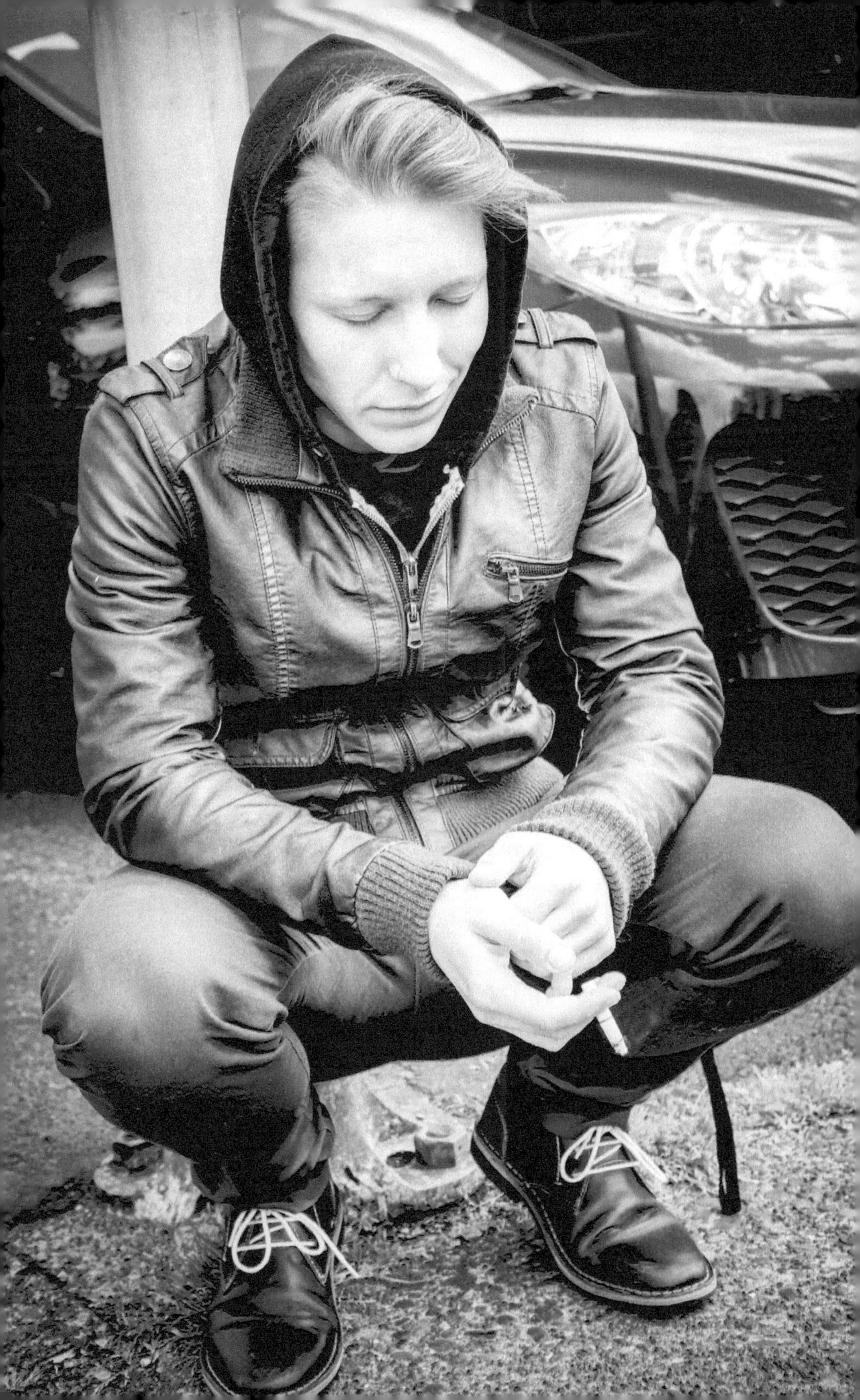

THE AUTHOR PHOTO

I RECENTLY BOUGHT A COPY OF *MADAME BOVARY* IN PART because it is a book I have been meaning to re-read for a long time, but mostly because it had just appeared in a new translation, a translation done by one of my favorite contemporary writers, Lydia Davis—a woman who in her nontranslating life is the ex-wife of Paul Auster and the author of half a dozen wonderfully odd story collections. The first thing I did when I got the book was flip it open to the back cover looking for the author photo that invariably sits atop the bio these days. I found exactly what I was expecting—a picture of a woman I had never seen before. This is one of the many things that has, over the years, fascinated me about Ms. Davis—her author photos. I have never been able to identify the woman pictured on one of her books as being the same woman pictured on another, and I have wondered if perhaps this was not intentional—part of some artful effort to preserve a liberating anonymity.

There are a whole group of writers like this—Tim O'Brien being another example—who have dubious relationships to their photos, who seem to conspire with their portraitists to remain essentially unrecognizable. They stand in stark contrast to another group—those who have conspired not with their portraitists but with their publicists, those whose images have been quasi-copyrighted and have come to be, in part, physiognomic logos. Like Tom Wolfe—invariably portrayed as the quintessential dandy (so much so that one half expects to find him wearing an ascot when he showers). And Kurt Vonnegut who borrowed a large part of his trademark image and stage persona from Mark Twain. And most recently—though to a lesser degree—Jonathan Franzen with his serious horn-rimmed glasses.

Then, of course, there are the conspicuously missing pictures of Thomas Pynchon and J.D. Salinger and the deliberately disguised ones like Julie Hecht's. (On each of her books you will find the same distant shot of a skinny, blondish woman in sunglasses and baggy pants.)

Randall Jarrell once famously defined the "novel" as a prose narrative of a certain length with something wrong with it. The "author photo" can be similarly defined as a picture of a writer with something wrong with it. (You can test this hypothesis by pulling any five books at random from your shelves.)

For me, the best author photos are the ones that interfere least with my experience as a reader. A writer should look not only like a writer, but like an actual person as well—the sort of person who just might, on a good day, write the sort of book I might want to read. His or her photo should bear at least a passing resemblance to reality—if for no other reason than to suggest to the most easily duped of us a minimal sort of reverence for the idea of truth.

Getting these photos anywhere close to passable is a tricky business. There are so many things to consider: the pose, for example. There are the clichés to be avoided—first and foremost the chin-propped-on-the-fist thing (also known as The Thinker pose). It may be a classic that has been around since Egyptian times (and it may be a way to hide your neck), but today it just begs to be ridiculed.

Then, of course, there is one's expression—how to look thoughtful without looking grim, profound without looking pompous. And the perennial: to smile or not to smile. Generally it is frowned on. If one must smile then it should be done discreetly as it seems for each degree increase in a smile's wattage there is a corresponding degree decrease in the strength of the impression one makes as the possessor of a special sort of competence.

Along with the smiling issue, there is the hair issue. It shouldn't look too good. Like Amy Hempel's. It makes the would-be reader suspicious. Ideally an author should look like someone who doesn't care about how they look, like a substantive person who is concerned with significant things rather than trivial ones like appearance.

Most of my own author photos have been snapshots taken by my wife when we were on vacation. They're okay for what they are—casual, but not too insistently so. I am not pictured doing anything particularly quaint; I'm just standing there scowling a little like a slightly disgruntled lump (a thing that would definitely qualify, I think, as bearing a "passing resemblance to reality"). I would not object to some Photoshop shenanigans, to looking a little younger, handsomer, or smarter but I wouldn't want to look too much so as I am one of those people with a built-in hypocrisy-detector—the beeping would drive me crazy. I suppose if I had my druthers (yes, "druthers"), I would prefer something a little more candid. Maybe next time I can arrange to have something snapped from a duck blind.

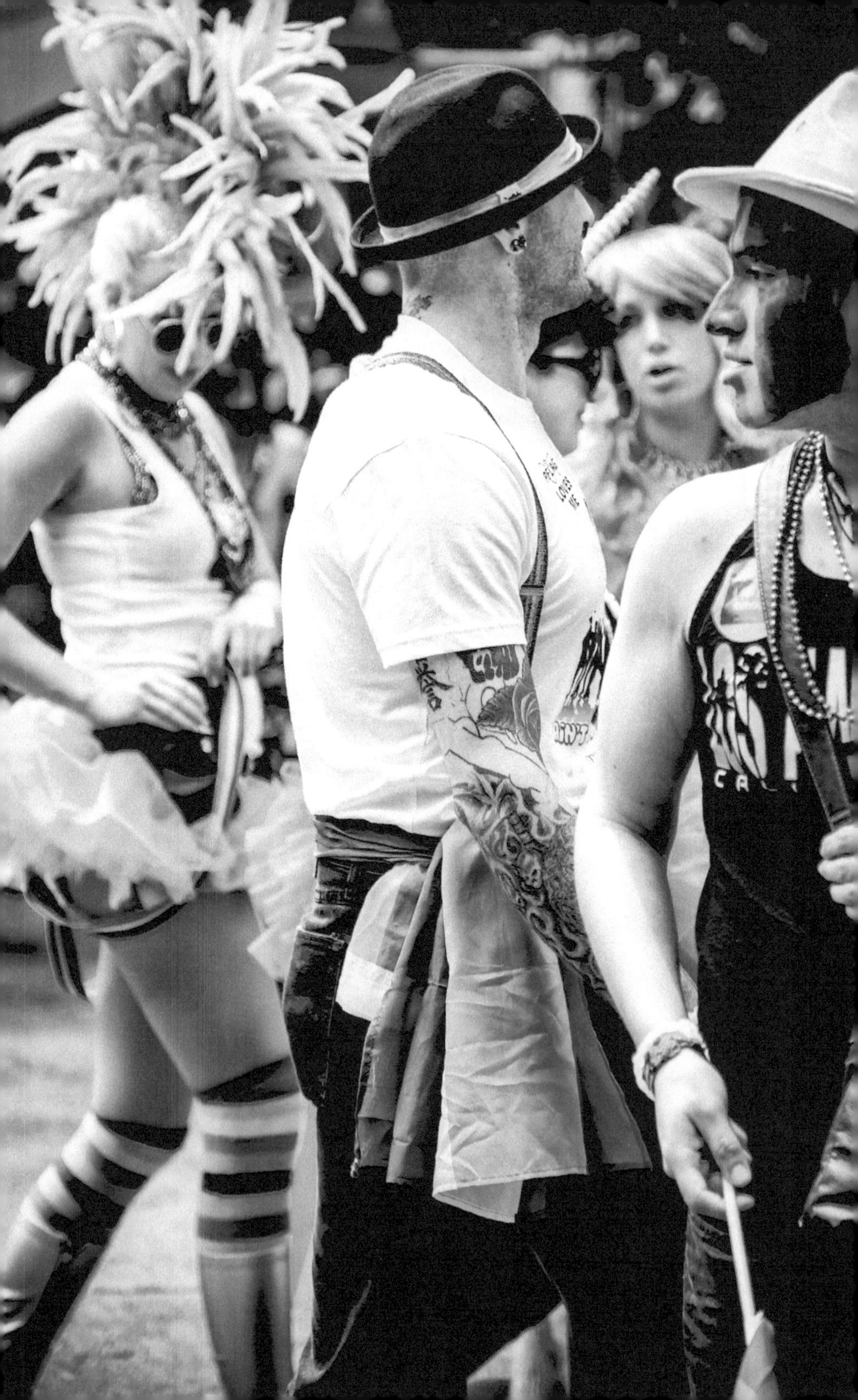

LOOKING AT GEOFF DYER LOOKING AT GARRY WINOGRAND

THE BOOK

Garry Winogrand was one of the four horsemen of the snapshot apocalypse. Along with Robert Frank; Lee Friedlander; and their champion, John Szarkowski, he introduced the world to a new photographic aesthetic, one that took the vernacular snapshot as its guiding inspiration. The critic Janet Malcolm found Winogrand's work "consistently and uniformly uninteresting." So do I. Geoff Dyer's work, on the other hand, is something else. A gifted and inventive writer, he is always worth paying attention to. His new book, *The Street Philosophy of Garry Winogrand*, is a personalized retrospective of Winogrand's work and an homage to two early books: John Szarkowski's *Atget* and *Looking*

Photo: Janus Face, 2013

at Photographs. Employing the same simple format of those books (one hundred photographs sitting face-to-face with an accompanying mini-essay), Dyer uses Winogrand's photographs as writing prompts—as opportunities to discuss work he admires and to free-associate, to roam imaginatively through literature, art, music, and movies.

The book itself is beautiful. Too beautiful. Wrapped in a tastefully embossed linen cover and lined with patterned end papers (referring directly to Winogrand's photograph on page 126), its relentlessly fastidious design sits in diametric opposition to its deliberately unkempt contents. The juxtaposition is jarring. It's like dressing a carp in haute couture.

THE PHOTOGRAPHS

The images Dyer has selected for the book are sequenced chronologically.

#1

A remarkable tableau staged by Chance, the patron saint of Photography. There are eleven subjects (thirteen if you include the baby and what looks like a chicken) arrayed like chess pieces on the front porch of a house in Kalamazoo. The year is 1958. A little quick to name-drop T.S. Eliot (and George Eliot as well), Dyer links this photograph to the early 1930s Depression-era images of the Farm Security Administration and to the work of Dorothea Lange in particular.

Dyer knows how to look at a photograph. He does

it extraordinarily well. One of the things he sees immediately (½ inch of train down in the lower left corner)
I missed at first glance. Unfortunately, some of the
other things he sees and comments on are not there
for readers of this book to see—for instance, a hidden
person, the word "Permit," and a house number (103).
Dyer is working from slides and prints while the hapless reader must make due with scanned images of a
lesser resolution. You can see a piece of paper, but you
cannot decipher the word "Permit" nor can you find
any house number. As for that missing person—I have a
guess where they are hiding, but it is only a guess. This
is a recurring issue that hobbles more than one essay.

#2

This mini-essay is particularly interesting because it
offers a quick look at what I have come to think of as the
standard features of a Dyer essay in general. It contains
an inspired and provocative connection (the relation of
the photograph [a bustling Manhattan street scene] to
history painting), important information (Winogrand's
abandonment of the long lens for the wide-angle), metic-
ulous observation (in the distance a "funereal" station
wagon with its trunk open), and a hair-mangling gust of
poeticized hot air ("the haze of the sky between build-
ings beckons like the end of history").

#3

Dyer, the ferocious observer, is counting bow ties and
using them in part to date a classic street scene from

the 1950s. The woman at the center of the image appears meek—"Her eyes...downcast like a geisha's." He "dyersects" the image astutely as a sociological and sartorial critique of the era's extant power dynamic.

#4

Here Dyer offers a pair of valuable observations: one about Winogrand's use of geometric shapes (more early in his career than later) and the other about his frequent use of the walking figure (who tends to be "vigorous and hurrying"). He refers to Winogrand as simply good old "Garry" and treats himself in an exiting paragraph to some harmless "Walker"/"walker" wordplay.

#5

"When Winogrand gets properly into his stride people [don't] know...what they are looking at or for." Dyer seems to think this is a good thing. "His pictures," he writes, are "an education in seeing."

#6

In thinking of Winogrand, Dyer finds himself (like the bronco buster in the essayed picture) riding another one of his favorite hobbyhorses: D.H. Lawrence. He quotes a tiresome passage from *The Rainbow* at length and suggests it might be useful as we look at more of Winogrand's work. I have my doubts.

#7

The children in this unimpressive photograph are, Dyer says, "straight out of Helen Levitt." It is an art history association like too many others. It assumes a viewer with a certain sort of education.

#8

Four men are examining a troubled car engine. It is an image that incites Dyer's return to the issue *de jour*—gender dynamics. It inspires him to quote a line from the poet James Lasdun's "A Jump Start": "last corner of our realm;/Machinery." This is followed by a bit of free-form fabulist flummery—a bicycle that "looks on curiously," a car with its hood opened, "a whale with a dental problem," and concludes with a typically wonderful observation—an unarticulated question that hovers over the picture: "Which of the four gallants in attendance knows most about cars?" Dead-Eye Dyer has an answer: "The hefty fellow in the white T-shirt." Why? "It's the cigarette that's the badge of honour: proof that he outranks his friends." This tell-tale cigarette that Dyer has spotted is barely more than a speck—a speck he is perfectly happy to hang his commentary from.

#9

"I am curious," Dyer writes, "about photographs by Winogrand featuring people I think look like other people." He thinks this man looks like an aged Neal Cassady—friend of Jack Kerouac and Ken Kesey. If you do not think he looks like an aged Neal Cassady, then much of what follows will be a waste of your time.

#10

If—like Janet Malcolm and myself—you find Winogrand's black-and-white work almost "uniformly uninteresting," it is unlikely you will be converted into a fan by his efforts in color. Here Dyer quotes Winogrand's most famous maxim: "I photograph to find out what something will look like photographed." It is a maxim that has, in its straightforward simplicity, endeared the photographer to many. Did Winogrand "see" in color? Dyer thinks he did. He thinks he photographed in color to see what something looked like photographed in color.

#11

A "great expanse of cliff, like Mount Rushmore... stripped of presidential carvings." "Cars, staring out to sea with their radiator grills serving as a toothy form of coastal defense." A Rorschachian reverie sent to rescue a pleasureless picture. When confronted with a certain sort of emptiness, the virtues of expediency become evident. Sheer explicative drivel is the besotted interpreter's only option.

#12

A photograph, Dyer says, from the golden age of sunbathing. "Not a tube of sunblock in sight." A typically ambiguous image, it allows our guide room to roam the associative backwaters of his literary fancy.

#13

An exaggerated angle of view, a pair of ceiling lights that look like eyes, a boxer throwing a punch, only the slightest portion of him seen in the catawampus frame—it is an image that takes a moment to sort. To me the "eye-lights" look cartoonish; to Dyer "god-like and all-seeing." His lexical momentum builds and once again carries him over the edge. Winogrand is the "agent and instrument" of a self-surveilling world, etc., etc.

Dyer closes this overheated essay with an ominous note about what is to come in Winogrand's later work. There Winogrand's "involvement in the picture-making process—framing, composition, editing—[will] be reduced," he says, "to less than the bare minimum." Randomness will rule.

#14

People lined up—it is a subject Winogrand says has always interested him. Here the line of people waiting to cross the street reminds Dyer of a police department's identity parade. His focus, however, is directed to "the tall, awkward fellow on the right." He identifies with this gangly boy, with "the beanpole nature of the metamorphosis he's undergone." While this group is obviously oppressed by the waiting, Dyer notes with astonishing sensitivity that "it is quite literally the *length* of the wait that [this slouching boy] embodies." Dyer's message to the temporally distant doppelganger: "Stand up straight. There are lots of tall women in the world."

#15

A frame within a frame—it is a peculiarly popular compositional tactic. I can guess why Dyer included this photograph (the "frame" being a signature Winogrand trope), but not why it failed to ignite his easily ignitable imagination the way so many other less-than-great photographs have. He obviously feels compelled to give us a certain number of words. Here, unfortunately, they do not add up to much.

#16

"Already, by 1960, Winogrand was taking pictures that didn't make any sense." Dyer responds here with a few paragraphs in kind. "The elbow [of a man scratching his head] is the element on which the whole picture hangs." Really? "I don't want to make too much of this," he says as he makes too much of it, "but once you start looking it seems that the cars have somehow sprouted elbows in the form of fins, as have the trees, in the form of branches."

Dyer returns to earth in his parting analysis of this complex scene: "The abundance of information is matched always by the amount withheld. In spite—and because—of everything that's going on, it's impossible to tell what's going on." This is noteworthy because this is the new grammar of photography, which is, of course, no grammar at all. It is the authentic, unintelligible, graceless babble of the real.

#17

When I read one of Dyer's mini-essays I am always expecting a surprise. I am expecting him to see something that I have not seen in my more casual, less affectionate scan. I am expecting him to say something uniquely his own, something original and revelatory. In three out of four instances this has been the case. Here is another example—an inventive discussion of continuity, of motifs, of how a representative cast of Winograndian characters (played by different actors) age, and of how in this specific instance the body language of these four women tell a "pre-feminist" story.

#18

A photographic mistake—an infelicitous misalignment awkwardly explained as preternatural orchestration. Not for the first time nor for the last Dyer gives credit when no credit is due.

#19

Dyer has some nice things to say about color. For instance, it is "more cinematic" and "in colour, people seem necessarily to be walking into the future (where the overwhelming bulk of photography will be in colour)." It adds, he says, "to the most earthbound or everyday scene." Yes, it adds, but does it add more than it subtracts? In most cases, no. Color is not for me what it is for our explicator: cosmic.

#20

A thirsty monkey, a can of beer, a box of half-eaten pizza. Dyer's enthusiasm for the color in this photograph is perplexing—unless, once again, he has been working from a slide or a print that is clearly superior to the reproduction in this book. A wider angle view of the very same shot in black and white (offered here as an accompanying insert) is a considerably more complex and engaging piece of work.

#21

Dyer compares and contrasts one of Winogrand's through-the-windshield photographs of "a classic or old-style pedestrian street scene" with modest reward to another through-the-windshield photograph—one in black and white by Dennis Hopper.

#22

"Muted." "Silent." "Featureless." "Beige." It is through sheer force of will that Dyer relates this parking garage to thrillers. He mines its relentless monotony for menace. "The lack of almost everything...makes the picture a kind of vacuum into which the potential for narrative is poised to whoosh"—and whoosh Dyer's narrative does, a narrative full of money drops, double-crosses, and espionage.

"The bulk of the image," Dyer writes, "is taken up by an expanse of pale bricks, the wall of the parking lot." This is an observation that focuses attention again on the quality of the reproductions in this book. This wall, as it is rendered here, is a solid, undifferentiated slab. For those positive about negative space, it will be the most delectable detail.

#23

Dyer dogpaddles around a particularly dull photograph—a fenced-in portion of tennis court—and finds, once again, a photographic particle (sunglasses) on which to pin an improv.

#24

With Dyer not all flights of fancy are created equal—some are antagonizing. This strained riff on monoliths seems little more than the silk-purse-out-of-a-sow's-ear exercise required of the contractually obligated.

#25

Charitably referred to by Dyer as one of Winogrand's "off-the-cuff" images, this melting block of ice sitting in the center of a sidewalk is seen as a chilling emblem of passing time. "The picture asks us that most Winograndian of questions," Dyer writes: "Why *this* moment? It holds our attention because it asks the question so slowly, and because it simultaneously declines to answer." I don't know about the asking "so slowly," but it seems to me this pair of sentences could (and probably should) appear on every page of this book.

#26/#27

Here are two street scenes (one black and white, one color) of people burdened by "stuff to be lifted and lugged, moved from place to place…suitcases, packages, and boxes." This is apparently a classic Winograndian leitmotif. Dyer's evocation of "Sisyphus" seems a little forced and high-falutin', but it is quickly forgotten when he focuses his talent for inspired and evocative similes on two of the men in the color photograph—"the ones hauling and guiding [the] rack of clothes like urban oxen pulling a plough through the concrete fields."

#28

This airport arrival sparks a Dyeresque commentary on social homogenization and the pointlessness of travel now.

#29

Suitcases and a half-page of half-hearted hokum.

#30

An image Dyer identifies perfectly as one of decision-making. A mother and her two children well-lit at the empty center of the frame are caught headed in different directions.

#31

A joyous greeting at the airport. The handmade sign says it all: "Welcome To California Jane." Dyer says more, of course, but he needn't have.

#32

A baseball player leaving Candlestick Park is surrounded by three boys hoping for autographs. It is one of Dyer's favorite photographs. He has expounded on it before. He is particularly interested in the boy whose glasses have been knocked off in the scrum. "This baseball player," Dyer writes, "becomes Winogrand's surrogate, bustling and striding through the world." The boy who has had his glasses knocked off is Dyer's surrogate. He is also, for Dyer, the most welcome of metaphors—a jumping-off spot for a quick myopic appreciation of Winogrand as the rebel who disrupted our conventional view of what a photograph should be.

#33

This store interior is stuffed with subjects, but Winogrand's central focus (and Dyer's) is on television—on a pile of kids sprawled on the store floor in front of a set of sets. It is a nostalgic picture, Dyer notes—one distinctly from another time, a time when staring transfixed at a screen was a communal rather than an individual activity.

#34

A parked convertible filled with people and a group of well-dressed passersby. Everyone in the car is looking to the rear. Something has happened outside the frame. It is, as always with Winogrand, impossible to say what. It is a photograph that Dyer chooses to talk about by talking about another photograph—one offered as another accompanying insert. This is something Dyer likes to do. It seems to me a bit of a cheat.

#35

The Winograndian mess is missing. In its place is a stark, static, well-composed picture of suburbia. Atmospherically it is, Dyer says "one of Winogrand's stillest images."

#36

Two well-dressed men waiting at the side of a dirt road in the middle of nowhere—an image that leads Dyer immediately into a discussion of Beckett's *Waiting for Godot*. It is an image, Dyer writes, "for an unwritten script and unmade film...about what's already been made, already been seen, already been photographed."

#37

An otherworldly barbeque at White Sands, New Mexico. A color image, it is too conventionally beautiful and well-composed to be Winogrand's—but it is. Dyer illuminates part of the central mystery when he notes an open car door and remarks on the absence of any sort of road. "There is nowhere to go," he writes, "or to have come from."

#38

"More waiting," says Dyer. More suitcases, too. They sit like birds on a wire—a pair of pilots and four stewardesses lined-up, legs crossed, on a long bench. "The absence of anything besides waiting is absolute. Floor, wall, bench—that's it."

#39

A crowded airport arrival. Dyer sees someone who he thinks looks like Bob Dylan, and away we go down the expository rabbit hole. Where we will stop, nobody knows.

#40

Yet another photograph taken in that least felicitous of places—the airport. A pair of men stand reflected in a window. As their images are doubled, so too are Dyer's efforts to excavate a response. What follows, I'm afraid, is a flight without a destination.

#41

No sooner does a straining Dyer exasperate (as in the previous text) than an inspired one enthralls. "The air itself in England in the 1960's looked older, gentler, more quaint," he writes. The occasion is a color image of Winogrand's—a park promenade featuring a set of grandparents minding a gaggle of grandchildren.

"Everything is subdued," Dyer says. "Even the gravel path is as soft as a beige cardigan." It is an affable ode to a not-particularly-interesting photograph, slightly chipped in the end by some departing twaddle about a time-traveling tricycle.

#42

An undeterminable number of people crammed into an absurdly small car—the sort of thing clowns pile out of at the circus. The obvious analogy for Dyer involves the Winograndian question of how much information can be stuffed into the photo frame.

#43

A pair of older ladies at a London mailbox and a few typeset inches of struggling folderol.

#44

I have a feeling this photograph was included by Dyer as a challenge to himself—a miserable thing to be insightful and entertaining about. He has hung his hopes on its peculiarities—the pointless pile of rugs, a desperately thin young girl.

#45

Winogrand and women—a tricky subject that has pro-voked Dyer's most voluminous response. This particular photograph was "taken in London on Kings Road, just west of Sloane Square," Dyer's old neighborhood. He "stood where Winogrand stood, hundreds of times."

#46

Another photograph taken along Kings Road. For Dyer it is old home week—and another opportunity to reference the documentary nature of Winogrand's work, his presentation of epochs past. Unfortunately, it is also an opportunity to add a dash of sheer rubbish about an antique taxi and its license plate.

#47

A skin-tight blouse and a fascinating excursion into art history—the evolution of perspective and composition in particular. The discussion revolves around Kurt Varnedoe's analysis of Edgar Degas and the radical new way of seeing found in his work—the oddness and dynamism introduced by the tilted picture plane and the capricious crop—features seen a century later as some of the defining ones of Garry Winogrand. "The precedent," Dyer says, "for the unprecedented."

#48

The rear end of a bus shot from a passing car. It is a simple image about which Dyer, the indefatigable truffle hunter, has plenty to say. It is evidence, he asserts, of one of Winogrand's central beliefs "that great photographs can present themselves at any time." No, it's not. This belief that great photographs may present themselves at any time is obviously true, but this is not a great photograph—it's not even a very good one. This belief that great photographs may present themselves at any time will "in the future," Dyer writes, "turn into a fatal and self-defeating addiction for [Winogrand]." Evidence of this fatal addiction can be found in much of his early work as well. There it is lauded and aestheticized.

#49

There is something about this photograph that stays with Dyer, but he can't say what. It is an admission I might have expected to be more frequent. "At a push," he writes, "I could have enlisted support from Milton to say that something about [the couple] harks back to Adam and Eve"—but that would be a push indeed. The couple in question, their arms around each other, are isolated by a telephoto lens and a shallow depth of field. Unusual for Winogrand. The embrace captured seems conciliatory. Dyer describes it perfectly: "in their huddled togetherness," he writes, "they closely resemble people in pictures of the aftermath of...bombings."

#50

A well-choreographed British street scene, "an English boozer where people stand outside the boozer, boozing"—a scene that makes Dyer both thirsty and homesick.

#51

This is one of the most un-Winograndian of Winogrand's phototgraphs. A touristy image of a leafy Hyde
Park, Dyer passed it up for inclusion in this book and
then reconsidered. As "a manicured vision of a mythic
past," it seemed to him the pastoral embodiment of an
expat's dreams.

#52

We return to airports. Here a group of well-dressed
arrivals walk toward us through a futuristically featureless tunnel, through what Dyer identifies perfectly
as "the endless corridor of eternity itself."

#53

Color and pattern. A red polka-dot shirt. A black-and-
white houndstooth pants suit. This scheme was picked
up by overzealous designers of the book. (See polka-dot
and houndstooth endpapers.)

#54

Winogrand gives us an appliance store window. Dyer
gives us a short history of color television and a similarly short indictment of this much-indicted device.

#55

Here a shop assistant is posed awkwardly over a supine

mannequin. He is captured in a compromising and perverse position—one that Dyer makes the most of.

#56

A woman stares out from a phone booth, her expression distant and lonely. We can just see a slim book resting under the purse in front of her. Dyer, using slides or prints, has the advantage again. He can read the title on this book's spine (*The Woman Who Rode Away*). Given the quality of these reproductions, we cannot. The fact that the book is by D.H. Lawrence is not insignificant. It has something to do with the selection of this image as this particular writer is an obsession of Dyer's. His book *Out of Sheer Rage* is a comic account of his unsuccessful effort to write a Lawrence biography.

#57

A young "lost-looking" woman at the center of an anonymous event. She inspires Dyer to wander off narratively down his own yellow brick road.

#58

Dyer finds this photo fertile. I do not. Notably multiracial, it contains discreet groupings of whites, blacks, and Asians. As a consequence, it also contains innumerable opportunities for commonplace pontification.

#59

This laughing woman with an ice cream cone—an image of sheer joy—is one of Winogrand's most recognizable photographs. (His ghost can be seen as a reflection in the window behind her.) Dyer, having material available that we do not (contact sheets?) informs us that three other photographs of the same scene include "that dread figure, *the boyfriend*." Let's pretend he didn't tell us that.

#60

A young black man hurling an ambiguous yell at what (or who)—no one knows. Dyer festoons the image with a routine breeze through the issue of race and references to both Walt Whitman and James Joyce. He concludes with a characteristic whiff of whimsy. (The man in this photograph speaking to the woman in the previous one.)

#61

A gang fight in the park. One of those self-captioned images. The gang's name, "Savages," is emblazoned on a jacket in the foreground (together with a skull, of course, and a snake). "As it happens," Dyer writes, "Winogrand took relatively few pictures of actual fights. There are more of dances."

#62

Another image Dyer has been particularly fond of. It appeared in his book, *The Ongoing Moment*. The young woman putting money in the blind man's cup might be the actress Ali MacGraw "a couple of years before she broke the world's heart in *Love Story*." It is possible, but unimportant.

#63

This is the cover photograph of the book—a black woman in a red coat. What catches one's attention is not that the woman is beautiful (she is), but that the photograph itself is beautiful, which puts it at odds with the most basic Winogrand aesthetic.

#64

"An uncomplicated slice of mid-period Winograndia," Dyer says of this street scene. Uncomplicated and uninteresting. Four elderly women walking down a sidewalk that they share momentarily with a half-dozen bags of garbage.

#65

A young lady in shorts walks before an ogling "guard of honour"—two sailors and two Army PFCs. Dyer has had access to additional pictures of this scene. He again has information that is not available in the image before us. (The young woman, it seems, was part of a peace demonstration.)

#66

The phone booth is a popular Winograndian motif. The man in this one—his arm stretched out, his palm flat against the glass—would look trapped if not for the smile.

#67

Another phone booth. In this one a young woman. One leg is propped up causing her short skirt to fall back. Dyer tries to de-perv this picture by suggesting "there [is] a hint she knows" she is being photographed, "that she's playing her part in this loaded moment," but I don't think he is successful.

#68

The phone booth theme continues. This time half-in and half-out of the booth is the man himself—Garry Winogrand. The photograph was taken in 1967 by Winogrand's friend, Jonathan Brand. The face is familiar, but much younger than I am used to seeing it. The suit and tie—they are a shock. Dyer links Winogrand's work to Dickens and Balzac (via Tom Wolfe). "No one," he says, "surveyed the [social land-scape] as ravenously as [he]."

#69

Photographed from the back, this woman leans into a car through the passenger-side window. She is strug-gling with a large package just as Dyer is struggling here with a response.

#70

"Look behind you," one wants to say to the man in the foreground with the camera hanging around his neck. Behind him is a woman in a headscarf with her nose flamboyantly bandaged. (It's infectious, the Dyer method of photo review.) In this case the master wanders off in a different direction identifying this as a picture about relationships before he heads over to the high dive and leaps off.

#71

Nuns and crutches—a pair of Winogrand's favorite subjects. This particular image Dyer says "is so loaded with information it's difficult to tell which elements are essential—another way of saying they all are." It is also another way of saying none are—or why not just leave it all up to the beleaguered viewer. This critique is one of Dyer's more labored efforts, a game he is playing with himself, a test to see how much he can see.

#72

An ugly picture of an ugly scene—an elderly woman laying injured and slightly bloodied on the sidewalk. A nun tends to her. She, the elderly woman, is being studied by many and ignored by a few. Nothing here is improved by Dyer's forced discussion of "mythic figures."

#73

A naked man at the center of a demonstration. No

matter what Dyer has to say, no matter what respected texts he roams, no matter what synaptical rockets he may fire off—this is first and foremost a penis picture. I will refer in Dyeresque fashion to Wallace Stevens and his poem, *Anecdote of the Jar.* In the poem a jar, "and round it was," is set on a hill in Tennessee. It overwhelms the wilderness. "It took dominion every-where." So too does this man's diminutive penis. It is the star of the photograph. The demonstrators are sup-porting actors. Dyer's discussion of public vs. private, of inner-directed vs. other-directed is background music.

#74

Mess meets mess. A typically sloppy Winogrand shot of street garbage caught in a sudden wind—much to pedestrians' dismay.

#75

A long-haired man on a gurney is wheeled across a crowded sidewalk toward an ambulance. He is closely monitored by a herd of onlookers—a fact that elicits some fancy footwork from Dyer and a long look at looking.

#76

Another image of Winogrand's that has captured Dyer's attention before—not because of its strangeness (two young ladies in a park leaning back-to-back against a tree, one kissing her boyfriend, the other looking off forlornly), but because Dyer had seen an almost identical picture before, a picture of the same scene taken by Tod Papageorge who had been out shooting with Winogrand. The similarity of these images leads Dyer into a discussion of "style" and its relationship to "subject." "The fact that these pictures are almost identical forces us to attend to the smallest differences—of framing and lens—and their surprisingly disproportionate psychological ramifications," he writes.

#77

A police funeral with accompanying flags. At the center is a warm moment among officers. Again, nothing is quite what it seems.

#78

One of many pictures, Dyer says, "in which Winogrand photographs other photographers at work." This particular photographer—one of eight young people gathered around a park bench—is working on a picture of (what else?) the pretty girl. Dyer spends most of this page speculating about their various relationships.

#79

Two young women walk toward us down a park promenade. While they are dressed identically, they wear very different expressions. These expressions are presumably their reactions to being photographed by Winogrand. "Although invisible to us," Dyer writes, "Winogrand is often a participant in the action he records."

#80

A young lady in sunglasses sticks a curled serpent's tongue out at the photographer. It is a gesture Dyer sees as "a frank expression of sexual power and freedom, of contemptuously lascivious independence." It is an expression I see as a contemptuous and satiric one of demonic possession.

#81

We are back in the airport. A pair of well-dressed travelers are seated, talking while they wait for their plane. Dyer senses perfectly a subtle something in the woman's manner. "She is listening," he says, "but part of her is not listening."

#82

A Winograndian still life. Pitchers, mugs, and glasses of beer arrayed on a table. An ashtray holding a half-smoked cigarette as well. It is a picture that was taken in Austin, Texas, where "coincidentally...much of [Dyer's] book was written and a lot of beer was swilled by its author." The glasses, filled and empty to varying degrees, stand in for the missing drinkers. "Photography," Dyer writes, "is all about details, about specific truths. But the lesson of this photograph...is that, give or take a fight or two, one night's boozing is exactly like another." You hear in this observation the not-too-distant echo of autobiography.

#83

A wide-angle shot of a football game with all twenty-two players captured in motion. It is included here in large part because it gives Dyer the chance to talk about another later football game—one in which Winogrand (photographing from the sidelines) was seriously injured. Winogrand, Dyer says, "[would] never again be quite as quick on his feet."

#84

A dull photograph that sends Dyer off into the future for whimsical sustenance. "Certain pictures," he say, "are like illustrations of passages in novels that [are] still to be written." A fantasy and an extended quotation from a Ben Lerner novel follow. One has to respect Dyer's facility to invent even if the product of that invention is annoyance.

#85

Suitcases, an airport, seven phone booths—this is basically a photograph of a Winogrand theme park.

#86

A wearying photograph containing cars, the afternoon sun, a street corner, a tipped-over shopping cart, garbage, and three pedestrians. A "Boulevard of Broken Dreams" and blather.

#87

Eye contact with an unhappy down-and-outer seated at the edge of a garbage can on Hollywood's Walk of Fame. Unfortunately, Dyer's desperate critique (complete with fantasy dialogue) is decorated with an extended excremental metaphor.

#88

From out of nowhere a balanced photograph from Winogrand and a calorieless vamp on movie-making from Dyer.

#89

The large, headless, bare-backed foreground figure is confronted by a small, beseeching old woman. It is a freaky sort of photograph that leads Dyer directly to a discussion of Diane Arbus.

#90

A banal beach scene so spectacularly unimpressive that it tests the powers of the indefatigable Dyer.

#91

Here a shackled escape-artist wows a crowd at the beach. The image is a fertile, megaphonic metaphor—Winogrand breaks free "of the established idea of ... pictorial decorum."

#92

A zoo picture—and a wonderful one at that. Also, from Dyer a heartfelt appreciation of his old mentor, John Berger. "This book," Dyer writes, "is a belated gift from one of the countless readers and friends to whom you've given so much, for so long." (Sadly, John Berger, ninety, died before he could receive this present.)

#93

Dappled light is the bane of photography—and dappled this party-in-the-park scene is. "It's so dappled," Dyer says, "it looks camouflaged. People are merging into trees."

#94

A crowded airport lounge and, for Dyer, a prelude to Winogrand's fading talent. "The passengers are waiting to be transported, in huge numbers, across the river Styx."

#95

The dazed look on this young man's face sends Dyer off on a referential treasure hunt through Bob Dylan's lyrical archive.

#96

This older woman, her right eye heavily bandaged, a handkerchief held to her nose, is one of Winogrand's most widely recognized images. It is, Dyer says, "a devastating and crucial picture in Winogrand's oeuvre—one he was destined at some point to take." Dyer then surprises me by dismissing one of the figures in the photograph. "The man in shirt sleeves approaching the camera," he writes, "is irrelevant." This is a shocking assertion from Dyer. It is one he could have made often on his way through this book, but he did not.

#97

A random selection of questioning faces with Dyer dowsing the eternal mystery of identity.

#98

A contact sheet from the Ivar, a strip club where Winogrand took thousands of pictures. It prompts from Dyer a Darwinian exegesis of the primal urge.

#99

The Porsche on the left is leaving the frame. In the distance a blonde woman lies on the street. An example of Winogrand's dissipated late work. "Whether Winogrand saw the woman in the street is impossible to say," Dyer writes, "but we do know that he did not see her *in the photograph*." His vision was overwhelmed by his obsession. This was one of more than three-hundred thousand exposures he never examined.

#100

Disappointing. One would have hoped for a more

engaging or interesting image in conclusion. An old man struggling up a flight of stairs—it was not chosen for its inherent value, but for the possibilities it offered Dyer to extemporize. "It is tempting to suggest," he writes, "that in this picture we see Winogrand's spirit leaving his body." He was running out of time. "Diagnosed with cancer…on 8 February, 1984, he died less than six weeks later."

THE TAKEAWAY

I may not be particularly receptive to Winogrand's formless photographs, but I take pleasure frequently in Dyer's formless riffing on them. Many of Dyer's impetuous impromptus are like dreams, and like dreams are really only interesting to the dreamer (and maybe one or two octogenarianic Freudians). They are invariably self-indulgent and occasionally just show-offy, their aim being to amaze the reader with the fecundity of Dyer's imagination and the breadth of his education—but they are also intended as encouragements to the viewer to venture out in their own responses, to not be afraid of shoveling a little shinola in service to a noble cause: Art.

Dyer has given us a reasonable retrospective of an impossible-to-retrospect photorheic. It is for me, a Winogrand agnostic, pretty much all I need to know about this prosaic photographer. Aficionados will, I am sure, have their complaints—it is part of being an aficionado. They will want a broader, more comprehensive survey of the man and his work—but for the vast majority of those with just a passing interest, this over-dressed sampler should be more than sufficient.

APPENDICES

THE INVITATION

A Fantasy

Dᴇᴀʀ Rᴀɪɴʏ Dᴀʏ Gᴀʟʟᴇʀʏ,

I wanted to thank you for the invitation to submit work. I was surprised, flattered, and honored to be asked. I was also, I'm afraid, simultaneously bothered—bothered by the accompanying page of detailed instructions for making this submission. Those instructions were, I thought, rather lengthy; cold in tone; and, to be blunt, unnecessarily dictatorial. There was, for instance, your initial admonition. You said in an assertive boldface font that the photographs you were asking for should be submitted via a certain electronic submissions program. You told me if I did not have an account with that particular electronic entity, I would have to set one up. I do not have an account with the entity in question, and I do not want one. I am something of a Luddite when it comes to this sort of thing. I try to keep the setting-up of electronic accounts to a bare minimum as these sorts of accounts have a tendency to metastasize into nuisances at an alarming rate. I did, as you suggested, look at the "complete set of guidelines" that this submissions program offered. They were pretty much what I expected—an unfathomable mix of Geek and English. Life is short; time is valuable. Hours spent setting up accounts and learning how to operate them are hours wasted, hours that could be better spent almost any other way—at a coffee shop, in the shower, playing fetch with my imaginary dog (a Labrador named Lucy).

You say in the invitation that you have secured the services of renowned photographer Stephanie Beach in the sifting and judging of submissions. I wish this was the good news you intended it to be, but it is not. It will assure some, of course, that certain standards are being met; it assures me—or almost assures me—of being rejected. I know Ms. Beach's work. I am not an enthusiast. I think of it as disingenuous, as a "playing possum" sort of photography, a photography that seeks attention by appearing not to seek attention. It offers a mock modesty that is informed by her famous mentor's aggressively understated dramas of daily dullness. She, like he, is committed to the photograph of nothing. It is a difficult subject. Few do it well. Most acolytes end up iffy. Her pictures are not about the world, but about photography—an interpretation of the "non-style" style, an aesthetic doctrinally hostile to the idea of "visual interest." I cannot imagine she would be receptive to my work which openly courts such an interest.

What would it be like to have my sharply focused, contrasty, conscientiously composed photographs hanging in the Rainy Day Gallery? In most ways it would be like having them hang in the galleries they have hung in before—in X, Y, and Z. The walls are the same chalk white, the germless spaces similarly configured—but given RDG's remarkable reputation, its aura of preeminence, I imagine the chances for recognition and sales would be infinitely greater. The prices for work hanging on your walls are considerably higher than the prices for work hanging on other, lesser walls. With a single sale I would have enough (after your commission) to buy that new pair of snow boots I've been looking at. But why imagine selling just one picture? That seems like the waste of a fantasy. Why not imagine selling the majority of them—or all of them, for that matter? If that were the case I could, perhaps, retire from commercial photography, from corporate portraiture. It is not congenial work. It keeps the lights on as they say— but that is only in the house. In me they dim. I am not an affiliative type. I score terribly on personality tests. (Conscientious, unstable, socially detached.) But why stop with my retirement from commercial portraiture? Why not imagine being freed from the usual career-building humbuggery—from the conferences, the workshops, the portfolio reviews, the shoulder-rubbing with "helpful" peers?

It is, of course, much easier to imagine my submission not being selected. I wouldn't be happy about it, but I would not be as upset as might be conventionally thought. As an aging realist my reactions to acceptance and rejection have grown steadily more muted. The excitement of one and the disappointment of the other have been getting shorter and shorter lived. There would be no grief counselors required, no candlelight vigils. I would console myself with an average bottle of wine (rather than something special), a recorded episode of *Inspector Morse*, and the knowledge that I had avoided the odious obligation of an artist's talk. (I have visceral dread of that particular convention. My spirits—which are rarely that high in the first place—plummet at the thought of these gilded sales pitches.)

———

I know this letter is late, and for that I apologize, but your request for this submission arrived just as I was packing for a trip to Chicago and I did not think I could give it the attention it deserved, which, as it turns out, was unfortunate because I worried the whole time I was away that the delay in my response would be judged offensive and misinterpreted by you as a lack of regard. This worry ruined much of my fun in Chicago. It interrupted my contemplation of *Paris Streets*, Caillebotte's famous painting at the Art Institute. It was much larger than I expected, which, of course, started me thinking about the issue of "scale," which, in turn, started me thinking yet again about your invitation with its curt directive regarding print size.

You say if a submission is selected for exhibition, the

printed images—which must be identical to the images offered via electronic submission ("ABSOLUTELY NO SUBSTITUTIONS PERMITTED")—should be delivered to the gallery matted and framed. You say they should not exceed such and such number of inches one way nor such and such number of inches the other. I am not an obstinate person, but neither am I a reflexively pliant one. I understand this is a special program; that it is separate from normal gallery operations; that those of us who have been invited to submit form a subgroup of some type; that we have not been chosen to join your stable of represented artists; that our work will not hang in the front gallery, but in one of the smaller back galleries; and, as a consequence, there may be some logistical issues involved, but this preemptive prescription with regard to print size (down to the one-half inch) seems to me, at the very least, presumptuous. These are issues that should be the photographer's to struggle with as they relate directly to aesthetic intent.

—

I have a number of other things I would like to discuss with you in regard to a submission, but I am afraid I must cut this note short. I am photographing an insurance salesman in about an hour, and he is on the other side of town. He wants to update a portrait I did of him two years ago. (He has grown a beard and is convinced that it lends him a new monetizable gravitas.) I will be tempted, as always, to take the sort of photograph I want to take (something resonantly real), but I won't because I know from past experience my client will complain that the image is not flattering. So it will be the usual thing: ten minutes, seamless backdrop, standard three-light set-up—not a portrait, but a grinning widget.

I know you are waiting for my reply to your generous invitation and that you have a very specific deadline for this reply, but I feel I must ask for an extension. At the moment I am leaning one way, and I hope (perhaps soon) to be leaning another. If an extension is impossible, I understand. I will say again, it was an honor to be considered.

All the best,
Yrs. sincerely
Etc., Etc.

CAPTIONS

A Short Story

ABOVE: A PORTRAIT OF PHILLIP HILLWOOD PAINTED BY the doddering and much-acclaimed expressionist Malcolm Ulrich appeared in conjunction with a breathless story titled "Painters of Promise" on the cover of *Modern Movement* magazine's March 12, 1985, issue.

Right: Hillwood's French dealer and amatory correspondent, Yvette Bucci.

Above: Hillwood made his first trip to France in 1985. He was converted, he said, from Anglophilia to

Francophilia in a matter of minutes. "I left the airport in Paris feeling one way and arrived at my hotel in Montparnasse feeling another. I was possessed."

—

Top: An intoxicated Hillwood at a symposium in Carmel on "The Future of the Figure in Postmodern Painting." He and his fellow symposiasts had not come for the topic (which they ignored), but for the seaside sabbatical. Hopkins spoke on the psychology of color; Coleman on the act of painting; and Miller (second from the right), who idolized Hillwood, spoke on Nietzsche and narcissism.

—

Left: Wryson, Hillwood, and Jasper Johns.

—

Bottom Left: Amelia Coyne at home in Cannon Beach, 1986

—

Left: Director Anton Evans, actor Alex Eskenazi, and Hillwood on stage before rehearsals of *A Long Day's*

Journey into Night—Hillwood's first and last foray into set design.

—

Right: Hillwood working on an irreverent interpretation of Ingres.

—

Below: Hillwood in front of Seattle's Pike Street Market. "It is an almost perfect city," he said of his hometown. "Big, temperate, on the water, and 1200 miles away from Los Angeles."

—

Right: Hillwood and his twelve-year-old son, Michael, a budding moralist. Michael kept an eye on his father's drinking and for a time strove to be his conscience.

—

Right: Misjudging a leap from a stone wall near his home, Hillwood tore ligaments in his left knee a month before his *Winterscape* show at the Seattle Art Museum. "I hoped the persistent physical pain would distract me from worry about the show," he wrote to a friend, "but this has not been the case."

Left: Michael and his father canoeing on Lost Lake.

Below: Hillwood, Michael, and wife Maureen (in polka-dot dress and unfortunate hairdo) traveled to Milan for the International Imagist Conference in 1991.

Right: Dena Malcolm. Hillwood described her as "the sort of person who actually enjoys reading Henry James, the sort of person who owns a copy of *The Golden Bowl*."

Above: Hillwood at age seven dressed as Zorro. This photograph appeared on a Christmas card that Hillwood sent out in 1992.

Left: Hillwood playing pool. He could never pass up the chance to chalk a cue.

—

Left: Hillwood adored Karen Wheeler. He treated her as if she were a surrogate daughter—a fact that did not go unnoticed (or unremarked upon) by Hillwood's non-surrogate children who would have welcomed, if even just occasionally, similar displays of affection.

—

Right: Hillwood and Raymond Perry in San Diego, 1993. Perry, who was famous in part for being unapologetically alcoholic, was amazed at how much Hillwood drank. The two promoted each other professionally and became friends.

—

Left: Hillwood at a costume party in the middle nineties.

—

Left: Hillwood and family with Ben Brett, a photographer, who was for a while one of Hillwood's closest

friends. Clockwise from the top: Amy with Hillwood's son John, Maureen and grandson Dylan, Michael, Brett, and Hillwood.

—

Bottom Left: Maureen and Phillip on a picnic in Oaks Park.

—

Left: Peter Westbrook spent more than a year working on his profile of Hillwood for *The New Wave*. He and Hillwood were friends until June 15, 1999, when the profile was published.

—

Right: Alice Mayor at Bond House, a painters' retreat, 1995. "An unreconstructed temptress," Hillwood wrote.

—

Left: A despondent and conspicuously bare-footed Hillwood in the bleak-chic apartment on Farmington Road where he lived from 1995 to 1996 while teaching at Morton College. "It is the sort of place you might expect to end up if you had been living the life of a petty criminal," he told friends.

⌐

Hillwood, bored with his old Seattle clique, went out of his way to befriend younger artists such as novelist Marc Davies (*above*) and sculptor Ian Trapp (*left*).

⌐

Hillwood's seascape, *Unsettled*, was sold in April 1998 to the Metropolitan a week before he appeared on the cover of *American Painting*.

⌐

Above: Rebecca interviewed her father for the *American Painting* cover story. "I would have to say that I have had more than one encounter, Becks, but fewer than seems conventionally imagined," he replied when asked about persistent rumors of rampant philandering.

⌐

Left: Hillwood and Eric Fischl playing backgammon in Belgium.

—

Left: Trevor Hampton, critic for *Miscellaneous*, who described Hillwood's austere landscape *Cypress Grove* as "marred by an unmetabolizeable thanklessness."

—

Above: Sabia Green and Hillwood study a Matisse.

—

Below: Hillwood, uncomfortable in his rented tuxedo, presents the Gold Medal of Honor to Jonathan Newhall at the National Arts Club. "Jonathan is for real," he wrote to Ray Perry. "It has never been about the jewelry for him."

—

Left: Hillwood (in his "special" bow tie) receiving an honorary degree from Harvard in June 1999.

—

Above: Hillwood at the Washington State Fair.

—

Right: Hillwood won the 2000 National Art Critics Association Award. He appears here with fellow winners Lucy Goddard and Peter Mead. "It is an honor" he said, "but to tell you the truth, when I see someone like me get something like this I can't help but wonder who on the committee owed whom a favor and for what."

Left: In 2000 the Italian government provided Hillwood with a nubile young interpreter, Gabriella.

Left: "I think he'd be better employed plastering sheetrock," Hillwood said of portraitist Anthony Jackson. "I was worried that he might reveal something about me that I would rather not be revealed, but he has revealed nothing—except perhaps that my judgment isn't what it should be in that I did not refuse the request to sit for this."

Left: Carving the Thanksgiving turkey was a ritual that Hillwood took very seriously.

Above and left: Hillwood never cared for public lecturing. He did as little of it as he could. "I suppose it is good for me—like exercise; but, like exercise, I find myself avoiding it whenever I can," he said.

—

Right: Hillwood in a convertible that he bought with proceeds from the windfall sale of *Tintoretto Paraphrase*.

—

Right: One of Hillwood's consistent complaints about Phillip Shelly was that his "important" pictures were programmatic, that they "invariably contained three female nudes and something on fire."

—

Below: Chloe Hunt, one of Hillwood's young distractions, was drunk when she drove her car into the corner of a convenience store. Hillwood paid for her dental work and for the surgery that restored her nose.

—

Left: Hillwood and Rebecca shortly after she published her first novel, *Whatever Happens*. Hillwood was

relieved to find that he was not in it, that the heroine's father was a documentary filmmaker with a passion for social justice and not (as he put it) "a difficult old dauber who was impossible to deal with."

—

Right: Hillwood in the fall of 2002. He had been diagnosed with cancer three weeks before.

—

Left: Dogs were always a great comfort to Hillwood.

—

Left: Andrew Wryson delivers the eulogy at Hillwood's funeral in Port Townsend, Washington.

—

Right: After the funeral.

—

Left: Pallbearers (on left side of casket) included Michael, John, and Jeremy Thaw (wearing porkpie hat).

AUTHOR BIO

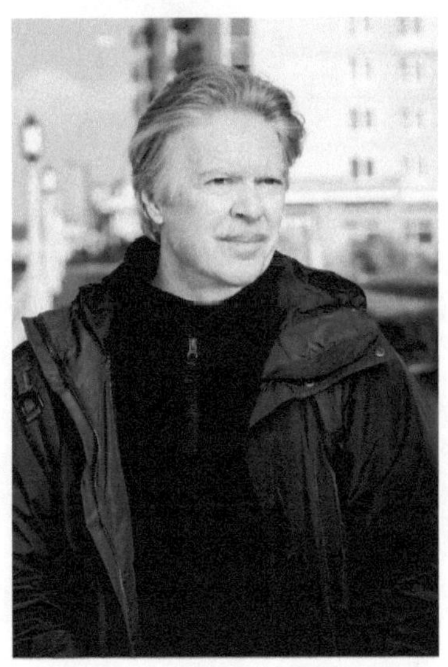

K. B. Dixon's work has appeared in numerous magazines, newspapers, and journals. The recipient of an OAC Individual Artist Fellowship Award, he is the winner of both the Next Generation Indie Book Award and the Eric Hoffer Book Award. He is the author of seven novels: *The Sum of His Syndromes*, *Andrew (A to Z)*, *A Painter's Life*, *The Ingram Interview*, *The Photo Album*, *Novel Ideas*, and *Notes* as well as the short story collection, *My Desk and I*. Examples of his photographic work may be found in private collections, juried exhibitions, online galleries, and at K.B. Dixon Images. He is represented by Michael Parsons Fine Art, Portland, Oregon.